FRENCH LANDSCAPE

English Channel

Atlantic Ocean

Mediterranean Sea

SPAIN

F R A N C E

Calais
Gravelines
Pourville • Dieppe
Le Havre
Grandcamp • • Honfleur • Les Andelys
Port-en-Bessin • Giverny
Montgeroult
La Rue-des-Bois
Paris
Etang-la-Ville
Rennes
Fontainebleau
Pont-Aven
Le Pouldu
Diénay • Dijon
Lyons
Bordeaux
Saint-Rémy-de-Provence • Aix-en-Provence
Nice
Gardanne • Saint-Raphaël
Arles • L'Estaque
La Ciotat
Saint-Tropez
Sète
Marseilles
Collioure
Barcelona
Horta de Ebro

Magdalena Dabrowski

French Landscape

THE MODERN VISION

1880–1920

THE MUSEUM OF MODERN ART, NEW YORK

Distributed by Harry N. Abrams, Inc., New York

Published on the occasion of the exhibition **French Landscape: The Modern Vision, 1880–1920**, organized by Magdalena Dabrowski, Senior Curator, Department of Drawings, The Museum of Modern Art, New York, October 27, 1999–March 14, 2000. **French Landscape** is part of a larger exhibition, **Modern*Starts***, which is in turn part of a cycle of exhibitions entitled *MoMA2000*.

This exhibition is part of *MoMA2000*, which is made possible by The Starr Foundation.

Generous support is provided by Agnes Gund and Daniel Shapiro in memory of Louise Reinhardt Smith.

The Museum gratefully acknowledges the assistance of the Contemporary Exhibition Fund of The Museum of Modern Art, established with gifts from Lily Auchincloss, Agnes Gund and Daniel Shapiro, and Jo Carole and Ronald S. Lauder.

Additional funding is provided by the National Endowment for the Arts and The Contemporary Arts Council of The Museum of Modern Art.

Produced by the Department of Publications, The Museum of Modern Art, New York

Edited by David Frankel
Designed by Ed Pusz with Emily Waters
Production by Christopher Zichello
Printed and bound by Stamperia Valdonega S.R.L., Verona

This book was set in Emigre Mrs. Eaves, designed by Zuzana Licko, and in FontShop Scala Sans, designed by Martin Majoor. The paper is Larius Matte Satin by Cartiere Burgo.

Published by The Museum of Modern Art
11 West 53 Street, New York, New York 10019
(www.moma.org)

Distributed in the United States and Canada by Harry N. Abrams, Inc., New York (www.abramsbooks.com)
Distributed outside the United States and Canada by Thames & Hudson, Ltd, London

Library of Congress Catalogue Card Number: 99-75009
ISBN 0-87070-027-8 (MoMA, Thames & Hudson)
ISBN 0-8109-6204-7 (Abrams)

COVER, TOP: Vincent van Gogh. **The Olive Trees** (detail). 1889. Oil on canvas, 28 5/8 x 36" (72.6 x 91.4 cm). The Museum of Modern Art, New York. Mrs. John Hay Whitney Bequest. COVER, BOTTOM: **Mont Gaussier, Provence**, 1986. Photograph: Jean Delrieux. FRONTISPIECE: Nickolas Muray. **Garden of Claude Monet, Giverny, France**. n.d. Gelatin silver print, 13 1/4 x 10 1/4" (33.5 x 26 cm). The Museum of Modern Art, New York

Printed in Italy

TABLE OF CONTENTS

PREFACE AND ACKNOWLEDGMENTS

French Landscape: The Modern Vision, 1880–1920 is part of a cycle of exhibitions, *MoMA2000*, that focuses on the collections of The Museum of Modern Art, exploring their rich-ness in a fresh cross-disciplinary way. This particular exhibition includes works in the mediums that are the concentration of four of the Museum's six curatorial depart-ments: Painting and Sculpture, Drawings, Prints and Illustrated Books, and Photography. It comes to fruition through the collaboration and support of many on the Museum staff, in many of the Museum's departments: Painting and Sculpture, Drawings, Prints and Illustrated Books, Photography, the office of the Chief Curator at Large, Publications, Graphics, Photographic Services and Permissions, Exhibition Design, Registration, Operations, and more. The individuals to whom I owe a debt of gratitude include Nancy Adelson, M. Darsie Alexander, George Bareford, Kathy Bartlett, Mikki Carpenter, Anne Carter, Elaine Cohen, Kathleen Curry, Sharon Dec, John Elderfield, Chris Engel, Sarah Ganz, Thomas Griesel, Sarah Hermanson, Christel Hollevoet, Linda Karsteter-Stubbs, Kate Keller, Michael Maegraith, Elaine Mehalakes, Jerry Neuner, Peter Perez, Ed Pusz, Peter Reed, Gina Rossi, Kirk Varnedoe, John Wronn, Michelle Yun, and Chris Zichello. There were also those outside the Museum staff who contributed to the book in different ways; they include Jean Delrieux, Richard Kendall, Emilie Michaud-Janin, Susan Richmond, and Emily Waters.

I would like to thank Glenn D. Lowry, the Museum's Director, for his support of the project, and Jennifer Russell for her assistance in making it happen. I would also like to mention three people whose contribution I most appreciated: Veronique Chagnon-Burke, Mary Chan, and Angela C. Lange. They provided vital support in the most crucial aspects of the project, with great intelligence, and gave generously of their time and commitment. I am particularly grateful to my editor, David Frankel, whose skill and professionalism under the pressures of impossible deadlines made this book much more complete.

Outside The Museum of Modern Art I would like to acknowledge William Rubin, the Director Emeritus of the Department of Painting and Sculpture, for his contribu-tion to the exhibition. I must also express my appreciation for the generosity of donors whose works will enrich our collections in the future: Mrs. Melville Wakeman Hall, Janice Levin, David Rockefeller, and Sylvia Slivka. I owe them a deep debt of gratitude.

—MAGDALENA DABROWSKI

INTRODUCTION

In the late nineteenth century, landscape painting became a crucial medium of modern art. Only a hundred years or so before, the French had considered landscape a minor genre; although it had occupied a central place among the arts of Italy and of northern countries such as Holland, in France it was thought to lack the status of history painting or portraiture, both of which were recognized by the Académie as the "noble" manners of artistic expression. In 1800, however, the painter Pierre-Henri de Valenciennes, who had studied in Italy, published a treatise arguing for landscape as the equal of the other genres, and stressing the importance of sketching directly from nature.[1] In 1817, the Académie finally recognized the category and in fact established a Prix de Rome for it, a prize that would be awarded for the next forty-five years. Beginning in the mid-1820s, several further essays on landscape were published, bringing the subject to more general public attention.[2] The practice of sketching out-of-doors—*en plein air*—that Valenciennes had advocated grew steadily more popular, as artists such as Camille Corot began to draw notations of light and atmosphere that they would later transpose into finished paintings in the studio.

Despite the increasing prominence and importance of landscape art, it was not until 1848 that "pure" landscape was exhibited at the Salon, that imprimatur of acceptance by the art establishment and the period's primary forum for the presentation of contemporary art. By the 1860s, however, landscape painting had become enormously popular, and by a decade or so later it had become a vehicle of modernist innovation—this although it might to later eyes seem conservative by nature (since it is inescapably descriptive and essentially narrative, qualities frowned on by many twentieth-century modernists). The role of landscape in painting as a whole remained a topic for debate: what was to be depicted, and how? The generally accepted view was that a landscape was a depiction of nature without figures, or at least in which figures played a subordinate role. In 1861, the writer Maxime du Camp described such depictions as the best opportunity for "direct communion with nature," since the absence of figures induced a feeling of solitude. He also noted that the landscape was not just a subject matter but, more important, involved a way of seeing outdoor scenery.[3]

1. See Pierre-Henri de Valenciennes, "Réflexions et conseils à un élève sur la peinture et particulièrement sur le genre du paysage," *Éléments de perspective practique à l'usage des artistes*, 1800 (reprint ed. Geneva: Minkoff, 1973). For Valenciennes, the best-possible imitation of nature is the ideal that artists should seek, and has been since the classical era. He prescribes ways of composing landscapes and depicting features within them, taking into account the seasons and times of day; and he discusses different genres of landscape—the pastoral, the marine, the battle landscape, and so on.

2. See K. S. Champa et al., *The Rise of Landscape Painting in France: Corot to Monet* (Manchester, N.H.: Currier Gallery of Art, 1991), pp. 15–21.

3. Maxime du Camp, *Le Salon de 1861* (Paris, 1861), pp. 145–46.

The landscapes approved by the Salon were at first and for the most part safely Neoclassical in style. During the "liberal" phase of the Second Empire, in the 1860s, landscape art was much *en vogue*, and examples of it were often acquired by the French state; but these, too, were mainly tame rural scenes. Between 1860 and 1890, however, large events took place in the French political arena, of which the Franco-Prussian War in 1870, and the consequent fall of the Second Empire, were only the most obvious. The country was rapidly changing, and changes in art, previously kept to the margins, could no longer be suppressed. In fact art—and often it was landscape art—became a controversial emblem of social change. The Impressionist experiments of the 1870s—small, informal paintings that viewed often mundane, "unpicturesque" modern scenes in unexpected ways, their lightly worked surfaces looking unfinished according to the standards of the time—were initially perceived as utterly subversive.

One reason landscape painting was controversial, of course, was its intricate involvement with the French sense of national identity. Discussing landscape as a "medium" rather than a "genre" of painting, W. J. T. Mitchell has emphasized the political and social aspects of landscape depictions; "Landscape," he writes, "is a natural scene mediated by culture. It is both a represented and a presented space, both a signifier and a signified, both a frame and what a frame contains, both a real place and its simulacrum, both a package and the commodity inside the package."[4] As such, according to Mitchell, landscape is a "fetishized commodity," emblematic of the social relations that it conceals.[5] It expresses not only value but meaning; it mediates between humanity and nature. But the crucial aspect of landscape painting in the later nineteenth century was that it required scrupulous observation from the artist, who began to study nature under different atmospheric conditions and from different viewpoints. Arising out of this concentration on the process of seeing, landscape art lent itself to the development of the modern vision.

This body of art should certainly be considered within its historical and cultural context, however, rather than for its formal qualities alone. It must, in other words, be seen in relation to the urbanization and industrialization that put such strong pressures on Western European culture in the nineteenth century, and to the newly hectic and intense notion of metropolitan life reflected, for example, in the novels of Balzac. An evolution in social attitudes was taking place: for a large segment of society, the understanding of nature as a refuge from the city was an emergent idea. "Land" was coming to be viewed as "countryside," a place of retreat and recreation. Landscape painting can be considered a conservative force, a means of fostering national identity, emphasizing regional differences while maintaining a sense of nationhood; yet in nineteenth-century France it was at the same time a democratic art, an opening on the domestic countryside that was becoming an ever more crucial resource for the urban masses. As the critic Jules Antoine Castagnary put it, landscape painting was an art of modern man, a respite from the stresses of urban life, and hence represented the fulfillment of the Republican dream. "This sudden spotlight on a genre that until recently was obscure," he wrote, this unexpected taste for scenes of bucolic nature and rustic life, has been explained in various ways. Everyone has agreed, however, that the principal cause resides in the supposed decline of our aging society. Because we prefer simple, familiar aspects of the country lit by our sun to linear arabesques of the human figure and artificially balanced groupings in heroic compositions, everybody seems to be speaking of the decadence of the French spirit. That accusation is poor in wisdom and rich in inexperience....Landscape art is definitively not the final passion of a senescent people, it is the first seizure of power on the part of a society that is reawakening.[6]

The practice of painting outdoors, *en plein air*, had been firmly established in France by the artists of the Barbizon School, beginning in the 1830s or so. In 1879, however, the state and the cultural establishment took formal steps to encourage it, through state purchases and inclusion in the Salon, and this decision had the effect of bringing contemporary life more into play as a source of motifs. Around 1880, the Impressionist influence began to penetrate even the Salon. Landscape art had already moved decisively out of the studio, demanding from the artist a sensitivity to site as experienced on the spot, as well as a physical exploration of the countryside—and this at a time when art's urban public was itself ever more likely to travel, and more interested in the experience of different places. For all of these reasons, landscape painting became an arena of major innovation in technique, style, and conceptual approach.

This innovation, practiced in different ways by successive generations of artists, reflected a new and changing relationship between artist and motif. As John House has written, "The landscape view of nature is not about the site itself, but about the image that is made of it, whether a memory, a photograph, a verbal description or a painting."[7] In nineteenth-century France, there were many ambiguities as to what constituted a "landscape." The discussion focused on issues still argued over today: was a landscape an aesthetic object, a commodified view of nature intended to provide the city-dweller with a vicarious pleasure in the outdoors, whose painted image he could admire in an exhibition or at home, as a substitute for real travel? Was it an empirical representation of a specific place? Should it be true to nature, replicating nature in all of its detail? Or, if the landscape painter was to do more than merely describe a particular place, as it was thought the photographer did, should the painting be a personal artistic vision, taking liberties with the motif depicted? Should it show a nature transformed through the artist's insight and temperament? Or should it suggest a generalized sense of nature, rather than being tied to a specific site? All of the artists of the period found their own answers to these questions, juggling such issues as the pictorial traditions on which they leaned, how much they transformed what they saw, the degree to which they "staged" the picture, and the desire to create novel pictorial solutions in defiance of old conventions.

4. W. J. T. Mitchell, ed., *Landscape and Power* (Chicago and London: The University of Chicago Press, 1994), p. 5.

5. Ibid., p. 15.

6. Jules Antoine Castagnary, *Salons (1857–1870)*, with a preface by Eugène Spuller (Paris: Bibliothèque-Charpentier, 1892), pp. 203–5.

7. John House, "Framing the Landscape," in House, ed., *Landscapes of France: Impressionism and Its Rivals*, exh. cat. (London: Hayward Gallery, 1995), p. 16.

TRADITION

A sense of the beauty of nature can be found in the verses of Homer, and the historical origins of Western landscape painting can be traced back to classical Greece and to Rome. But the genre of landscape that flourished in nineteenth-century France has a more recent ancestry, in the work of sixteenth-century Italian artists such as Giorgione (fig. 1) and Titian. These artists did not paint landscapes as such—they created historical, biblical, or mythological scenes, usually featuring the human figure, and with landscape as a backdrop—but those backdrops did combine their allegorical content with observation of nature, in which they suggested a power and a perfection.

Nineteenth-century French landscape painting effectively respected two subsequent streams of tradition, a southern and a northern. The first descended from the Neoclassical landscape type, the so-called *grande tradition* tracing back to the seventeenth-century Italianate scenes of Claude Lorrain and Nicolas Poussin (figs. 2 and 3). This line, and the earlier fusion of allegory and reality, was extended in the art of Jean-Antoine Watteau, whose *"fêtes galantes"* such as *A Pilgrimage to Cythera* (1717; fig. 4) were scenes of social gatherings in picturesque places. The Italian model offered several categories of landscape painting, depending on the motifs depicted and the visual spaces in which they appeared: the ideal, the heroic, the pastoral or arcadian, the beautiful, the picturesque. Strong in academic art throughout the nineteenth century, its legacy can also be seen in such works as Corot's "souvenirs," of the 1850s and 1860s (fig. 5).[8]

Other landscape artists, however, were effectively trying to subvert these traditional categories and to originate new conceptions of the genre. Their wellspring in these developments was a northern body of landscape art, contemporaneous with Lorrain and Poussin but produced in the Dutch and Flemish lowlands, and exemplified by the works of Meindert Hobbema and Jacob van Ruisdael (figs. 6 and 7). Where the Neoclassical landscape was idealized and arcadian, the Dutch was informal, domestic, and realistic. It entered the French tradition in the work of the Barbizon School.[9]

These originating paradigms, to whichever of them the artist clung, or however the artist mingled them, affected the composition of a painting, the choice of subject, and the selection of the viewpoint from which to depict the scene. Additionally, while drawing on the

FIGURE 1. Giorgione. **The Tempest.** c. 1505. Oil on canvas, 31 1/4 x 28 3/4 (79.4 x 73 cm). Galleria dell'Accademia, Venice

FIGURE 2. Claude Lorrain. ***Landscape with the Arch of Constantine.*** 1648. Oil on canvas, 38 9/16 x 58 7/16" (98 x 148.5 cm). Kunsthaus Zurich. Gift of the Holenia Trust in memory of Joseph H. Hirshhorn

FIGURE 3. Nicolas Poussin. ***Landscape with the Body of Phocion Carried Out of Athens.*** 1648. Oil on canvas, 44 7/8 x 68 7/8" (114 x 175 cm). National Museum of Wales, Cardiff. On loan from the Earl of Plymouth

different elements of the two traditions, artists were thinking more and more about the materiality of paint and canvas. Previous generations of painters had to a much greater degree subordinated the visual presence of their materials as materials to the creation of a convincing illusion; the viewers of late-nineteenth-century paintings, however, were increasingly made aware that they were looking at flat surfaces covered with colored pigment. Both the northern and southern traditions, meanwhile, had to be considerably stretched, historically as well as structurally, in order to reflect the conditions of modern life in any adequate way. The railways, for example—a new technology at the time—not only made the countryside more completely and more generally accessible but altered the way the countryside was viewed: seen from the window of a train, it became a rapidly changing flow of images, and the sense of its physical variety was heightened, since the traveler might cross a number of geographical regions within a few hours.

The arcadian landscape tradition—derived from Poussin, and from Claude's pastoral depictions of the Roman Campagna—was harder to sustain than the Dutch line, which passed, though transforming as it went, from the Barbizon on to the Impressionists and to Paul Cézanne. Yet Cézanne himself is said to have spoken of his desire "to redo Poussin after nature,"[10] suggesting a fusion of modern habits of observation with Poussin's classical sense of structure. And in the first decade of the twentieth century the arcadian vision definitively reemerged and melded with the more naturalistic approach. Henri Matisse's *Luxe, calme et volupté* (1904–05; fig. 8) and *Le Bonheur de vivre* (1905–06; fig. 9), the seminal examples respectively of his Neo-Impressionist and Fauve styles, combined the contemporary art of landscape with visions of a golden age, and reconciled the kind of innovation seen in Impressionist landscape painting with the *grande tradition*. By this time it was no longer appropriate to talk of the northern and the southern currents; landscape would now evolve in a more conceptual direction, in Cubism.

8. Champa et al., *The Rise of Landscape Painting in France*, p. 38.

9. On the Barbizon School see Robert Herbert, *Barbizon Revisited*, exh. cat. (New York: Clarke & Way, 1962), and Jean Bouret, *The Barbizon School and 19th Century French Landscape Painting* (Greenwich: New York Graphic Society, 1973).

10. See, for example, Richard Verdi, *Cézanne and Poussin: The Classical Vision of Landscape*, exh. cat. (Edinburgh: National Galleries of Scotland, in association with Lund Humphries, London, 1990), p. 57.

NATIONAL IDENTITY

French landscape painting may have been inspired by foreign traditions, but from at least the 1830s or so the landscape it made its subject was that of France. The rise of this art accompanied an intensification of national consciousness. After the fall of Napoleon, in 1815, a desire for national self-definition became extremely important in France; the idea of the fatherland—of "*la patrie*"—became a crucial issue.[11] The country was largely agrarian, and was seen by its people as defined by its fields and farms, its woods, rivers, and mountains; landscape art, then, was thought to have a particular relation, even a particular responsibility, to the fundamental character of France. The public grew increasingly interested in seeing and acquiring landscape images of many kinds; after around 1820, topographical prints and dioramas, made available by advances in the technology of printing, were widely collected, presaging the popularity of landscape photography within a few years after the invention of the medium, in 1839.

Under the Third Republic, after the fall of the Second Empire in 1870, an image of a rural peasant girl—"Marianne"—became a national symbol that remains alive to this day. Alongside Marianne there arose the idea of "*la belle France*." Critics, the audiences of the Salon, and average folk alike applauded pictures extolling the beauty of archetypal French countryside, and casting it as calm, domesticated, and harmonious. Such pictures, as Castagnary argued, enhanced their pride in being French, inheritors of a land worth commemorating in art. The spirit of a "*France profonde*," rooted in the soil, stood in opposition to the infringements of modernity so evident in the industrial towns of the north and east.

The countryside seemed increasingly tamed, increasingly imperiled by industrialization. Paintings of traditional rural life created an illusion of stability, sometimes reinforced by allusions to religion; Jean-François Millet's *Angelus* of 1855–57 (fig. 10), for example, shows humble peasants in prayer, apparently in communion with the land. Yet Millet's art made few concessions to earlier ideas of beauty. It was part

FIGURE 4. Jean-Antoine Watteau. *A Pilgrimage to Cythera.* 1717. Oil on canvas, 51 x 76 ¹/₂" (129.5 x 194.3 cm). Musée du Louvre, Paris

FIGURE 5. Camille Corot. *Souvenir of Mortefontaine.* 1864. Oil on canvas, 25⁵/₈ x 35" (65 x 89 cm). Musée du Louvre, Paris

of a realist movement, beginning in the 1840s and running through the next several decades, that emphasized meticulous observation of contemporary life.

Millet recognized that life in the countryside was actually harsh, and in fact was declining in quality. As regions gradually industrialized, a rising class of relatively wealthy tenant farmers replaced the traditional peasants as workers of the land. Meanwhile country people became increasingly dependent on urban services and goods, for small village industries were going out of business, the products they had supplied being more cheaply available as imports from the mass manufacturing plants of the cities. The results were rural unemployment and depopulation. The poorest laborers left to look for work in the cities, which, however, they often lacked the skills to obtain. Yet despite their discontent, the general prosperity under the Second Empire and then the Third Republic led many of these people to cast their political support to the state.

France actually remained primarily rural—its cities did not grow as fast as those of England, for instance. In 1866 only 11 percent of the population lived in cities of 50,000 or more; by 1890 that figure had doubled, but that still made for a predominantly agrarian nation.[12] Even so, by the second half of the nineteenth century the percentage of the land that could be considered wild and untouched had significantly decreased, and few places remained to give landscape artists the illusion that they could capture the unspoiled beauty and spirit of old France. The new landscape painting that emerged was unsentimental but also antirealist in its opposition to objective factual depiction. It attempted to resurrect or rediscover a premodern state of nature—to constitute "a visual reproduction of society in its natural setting," as Castagnary wrote.[13]

It has to be emphasized that a crucial feature of France during this period (and still today) was its diversity. Every region—Normandy, Brittany, Provence—was molded by its own history and geography, and car-

FIGURE 6. Meindert Hobbema. *Avenue at Middelharnis.* 1689. Oil on canvas, 41 x 55 1/2" (103.5 x 141 cm). National Gallery, London

FIGURE 7. Jacob van Ruisdael. *The Great Forest.* n.d. Oil on canvas, 54 7/8 x 70 7/8" (139.5 x 180 cm). Kunsthistorisches Museum, Vienna

11. See James McMillan, "La France Profonde, Modernity and National Identity," in House, ed., *Landscapes of France*, pp. 52–59, and Pierre Nora, ed., *Les Lieux de Memoire* (Paris: Gallimard, 1997), vols. 1–3.

12. See McMillan, "La France Profonde, Modernity and National Identity," p. 52; see also J. M. Merriman, *French Cities in the Nineteenth Century* (London: Hutchinson, 1982).

13. Castagnary, *Salons,* p. 187.

FIGURE 8. Henri Matisse. *Luxe, calme et volupté.* 1904–05. Oil on canvas, 38 3/4 x 46 1/2" (98.5 x 118.5 cm). Musée d'Orsay, Paris

FIGURE 9. Henri Matisse. *Le Bonheur de vivre.* 1905–06. Oil on canvas, 68 1/2 x 93 3/4" (174 x 238.1 cm). Barnes Foundation, Merion, Pa.

ried its own character: the Norman, the Celtic, the Mediterranean. These regional differences stimulated artistic creativity. Visually identifiable through architecture, scenery, and costume, they attracted artists philosophically as subject matter, but also offered possibilities for new pictorial vision.

TRAVEL AND TOURISM

The appreciation of landscape painting, and of the countryside itself, was closely allied to the expansion of the national railroad network connecting Paris to the provinces. As the possibilities of travel increased exponentially for people of every social class, there was a change in the *concept* of travel. People had always ventured abroad for business and trade; at least since the Age of Enlightenment, too, the wealthy had undertaken the "grand tour," visiting the historic sites and monuments of Italy, Greece, or Egypt to enhance their knowledge of past civilizations. Now, however, city dwellers right down to the level of the worker or petit bourgeois artisan could become day-trippers seeking rest and recreation in green fields or at the beach, experiencing nature in quick, short-lived bursts. The new means of transportation made open space newly accessible, and led to the emergence of a new kind of art collector: the urban resident who admired country scenery, and sought out celebrations of the gentle land of France.

The "*grandes lignes*," the railroads connecting Paris with the major French cities, were essentially completed by 1850. The first track out of Paris, to Saint-Germain, a few miles to the west, opened in 1837. Paris–Rouen followed in 1843, Paris–Le Havre in 1847. After the interconnection of the large urban centers, a broader, more local tissue of railway lines was constructed, beginning in the 1880s. As travel became a product for popular consumption, it also became a subject for art, in such works of social commentary as, for example, Honoré Daumier's *Third-Class Carriage* of c. 1862 (fig. 11). There was also an efflorescence in the publication of travel books and magazines, as the growing middle and working classes of the cities manifested an increasing desire to visit picturesque or historic sites and monuments. In paintings produced for the conservative Salon, ruins, churches, and châteaux were frequent subjects, extending the Romantic tradition and highlighting the emblems of history. More advanced artists—the Impressionists in the 1870s, the Neo-Impressionists the decade after—tended to favor depictions of a nature relatively untainted by human activity, at least in its modern forms.

The expansion of the railways decisively changed the profile of travel. The "traveler"—the voyager drawn to historic sites and cities, or to contemplate the sublimity of nature—was replaced by the "tourist," whose main purpose was to escape the pressures of the modern city by spending his limited free time in the countryside. Yet he generally visited the country amid a crowd of other urban folk. As France prospered, tourists were an increasing presence in its picturesque landscapes, which came to have a double life—both vehicles of nostalgia for premodern times and modern commodities in themselves. There came into being a leisure subculture, indeed a leisure industry, a mass phenomenon and a commercial investment. Recreation involving travel, now accessible to a large economic cross-section of French society, took an ever larger variety of forms—

FIGURE 10. Jean-François Millet. *The Angelus.* 1855–57. Oil on canvas, 21⁷/₈ x 26" (55.5 x 66 cm). Musée d'Orsay, Paris

day in the country, day at the races, day on the river, week in a coastal resort.

All of these activities were examined by artists, for instance Georges Seurat, in *Sunday Afternoon on the Island of La Grande Jatte* (1884–86; fig 12). Landscape here is the backdrop for leisure activities (among other functions), but landscape art proper focuses on landscape itself. In a world of growing tourism, the landscape artist was an antitourist, a traveler not only seeking sites of interest and beauty but trying to present them in a uniquely personal way.

The discussion of French landscape painting presented in this book is based entirely on the rich collections of The Museum of Modern Art, collections not only of paintings but of drawings, prints, and photographs. The landscape works in these different mediums are analyzed here for the first time as a separate group, exploring the different ways of describing the physical environment through those vital four decades of 1880–1920. (In the case of photography, the time frame has been made a little broader, since it seemed appropriate to chart a slightly wider range of the images produced in what was then a relatively new medium.)

The book is organized by geographic region. "Landscape art" is taken to encompass photographs of Paris streets by Eugène Atget and Jacques-Henri Lartigue as well as easel paintings made *en plein air*; the sites depicted run from Paris and its environs—places such as Fontainebleau, Montgeroult, and La Rue-des-Bois—to Brittany and Normandy, to more distant parts in the South, and even beyond French borders to the

FIGURE 11. Honoré Daumier. *Third-Class Carriage.* c. 1862. Oil on canvas, 25³/₄ x 35¹/₂" (65.4 x 90.2 cm). The Metropolitan Museum of Art, New York. Bequest of Mrs. H. O. Havemeyer, 1929

Catalonian village of Horta de Ebro, Spain, and to Morocco, both of which inspired outstanding contributions to the French tradition. The selection of art ranges from the work of Claude Monet, Cézanne, Vincent van Gogh, and Seurat, through the Fauvism of Matisse and André Derain, to the Cubist work of Pablo Picasso and Georges Braque; it also includes such rarely seen canvases as a marine by the Belgian artist Theo van Rysselberghe.

The works discussed represent new, individual attitudes toward landscape, different systems of representation, different content. The Impressionism of Monet, the Neo-Impressionism of Seurat, the solidly constructed landscapes of Cézanne—none of these renders a scene in anything like photographic terms. If the works' viewers want to know what the

FIGURE 12. Georges Seurat. ***Sunday Afternoon on the Island of La Grande Jatte.*** 1884–86. Oil on canvas, 6' 9" x 10' $^3/_8$" (208 x 308 cm). The Art Institute of Chicago. Helen Birch Bartlett Memorial Collection

artist saw, they must imagine it; the painting is a vehicle of interpretation. Ultimately, though, this is always true. The power of a landscape picture lies in its life as a metaphor, integrating or dislocating the compositional elements found in the local scene. The vitality of the landscape tradition lies in its power of adaptation and renewal.

From a purely formal point of view, the paintings and prints that follow introduce new attitudes toward the picture surface, emphasizing its expressive quality in differing ways. Landscape is represented here in terms of painterly effects; the contrast between painted surface and pictured depth is constantly stressed. In dealing with the basic relationship of figure to ground, the artists of this period moved decisively toward exploring the flatness of the picture plane. The Impressionists' dabs of paint in many colors, the Neo-Impressionists' application of color according to divisionist principles informed by scientific theory, the Synthetists' use of flat, unmodulated areas of color—all of these methods focus not only on landscape as mimetic representation but also on the landscape painting as physical object, and as a tool with which to symbolize the world. In their different ways, they both convey human concepts and values and reconfigure the traditions of pictorial construction. In some hands the manipulation of the elements of the painting can be interpreted as a political expression; according to James Herbert, for instance, the Fauve pastorals represent a combination of republicanism and Latin nationalism.[14] But whatever the method, it seems to be matched to the subject. It is our intention here to demonstrate the innovative aspects of the landscape art of the period, and the shifting aesthetic strategies of the artists who, in subverting the established traditions of the genre, also introduced the new languages of modernism.

14. See James D. Herbert, *Fauve Painting: The Making of Cultural Politics* (New Haven: Yale University Press, 1992).

PARIS

During the second half of the nineteenth century, Paris was transformed. The city had been a labyrinth of cramped streets and narrow Seine bridges, much of it unchanged since the Middle Ages. But when Napoleon III seized power and named himself emperor, in 1852, Europe was experiencing an extraordinary industrial and financial expansion, and this period of prosperity gave him the chance to become a builder on an imperial scale. With the help of his prefect Baron Georges Haussmann, Napoleon changed the face of Paris, effectively making it the "City of Lights" we know today.[1]

The changes included the demolition of old, unhealthy buildings to make room for elegant new neighborhoods and for a network of gas-lit broad avenues and widened streets. Ample parks were distributed around the city, creating green space for public recreation. Around the time of the Paris exposition, or world's fair, of 1855—the fair was attended by five million people, including thousands from the provinces and from abroad (among them Queen Victoria of England)—Haussmann also initiated a cheap system of public transportation. By 1867, when an American named Henry Tuckerman visited Paris after a twenty-year absence, the cosmopolitan nature of this modernizing city was clear: "The Gallic character," Tuckerman wrote in dismay, "...[has been] invaded and encroached upon by foreign elements....Baron Haussmann, the Prefect, has cut through streets, demolished whole quarters, made space and substituted modern elegance for old squalor."[2] Tuckerman was not the only one to rue the loss of the old capital of the Gallic genius; he had company in politicians and intellectuals at both ends of the political spectrum, from Victor Hugo to the Goncourt brothers.[3] But many of the more prosperous Parisians supported Haussmann's remapping, which, after all, gave concrete body to their prosperity.

It is the modernized Paris that we encounter in the work of Edouard Manet and the Impressionists. Manet's depictions of fashionable Parisians in cafés, restaurants, and theaters, Edgar Degas's scenes of men at the racetrack or outside the stock exchange, Claude Monet's views of the *grands boulevards* and Gustave Caillebotte's of the fresh-built bridges and squares (fig. 13)—all of these record the altered, smart (or at least *superficially* smart) Paris. Many of the artists were themselves relatively affluent members of the urban bourgeoisie, and some could be called *flâneurs*, a new type of fashionably

1. See Robert Herbert, *Impressionism: Art, Leisure and Parisian Society* (New Haven and London: Yale University Press, 1988), chapter 1, pp. 1–32, 307; David H. Pinkney, *Napoleon III and the Rebuilding of Paris* (Princeton: at the University Press, 1958); and T. J. Clark, *The Painting of Modern Life: Paris in the Art of Manet and His Followers* (New York: Alfred A. Knopf, 1985).

2. Henry Tuckerman, quoted in Herbert, *Impressionism*, p. 1, from Tuckerman, *Papers about Paris* (New York, 1867), p. 17.

3. See Clark, *The Painting of Modern Life*, pp. 36, 45, 47.

FIGURE 13. Gustave Caillebotte. *The Pont de l'Europe.* 1876. Oil on canvas, 49 x 71" (124.5 x 180.6 cm). Musée du Petit Palais, Geneva

dressed promenader devoted to the observation of contemporary life.[4] In their work, they often seem to embrace the life that was emerging in this city built on new sources of wealth, new forms of leisure, a new industrial and technological base. Yet they also depict worn and tired washerwomen, dancers exhausted offstage, lonely- and pensive-looking women in bars or at the theater—troubled, isolated people. The artists showed both sides of the period's prosperity, both the everyday pleasures of modernity and their costs.

As much as to painting, however, it is to photography that we owe our appreciation of both the old, now constricted or vanished Paris and the new.[5] Invented in 1839, photography was instantly popular. Just a decade or so later, Edouard-Denis Baldus was using the camera to document the monumental architecture of Paris, in images such as *Church of St. Germain l'Auxerrois* (c. 1850; plate 9) and *Bibliothèque Impériale, Nouveau Louvre, Paris* (1856–57; plate 8). Baldus's pictures were part of one of the more enlightened initiatives of the French state at mid-century, an effort to document the country's architectural patrimony photographically. The images produced in response to this campaign of course had to be informative, and a suitable documentary style developed in response to it, but the pictorial organization of Baldus's photographs, and his skill in capturing subtleties of light, make his pictures more than just functional records.

Charles Marville's *Rue du Cygne, Seen from rue Mondatour* (c. 1865; plate 5) offers a view of a relatively humble spot in the old city, a narrow cobblestoned street lined with rickety carts. Marville was documenting an aspect of the city's anonymous street life—a relatively hospitable anonymity, perhaps, next to the facelessness threatened in the so-called "Haussmannization" of Paris. Four panoramas made around the turn of the century, on the other hand (plates 1–4), show the heart of the new Paris—the Place de la Concorde and the Tuileries. Although both of these areas predated Napoleon's renovations, the unknown photographer's sense of them as grand, even grandiose public spaces—a conception reinforced by the wide panoramic views—is entirely consistent with Haussmann's vision. Another side of the new Paris appears in the work of Jacques-Henri Lartigue, who photographed fashionable folk patrolling the chic parks and boulevards of the modern city (plates 13 and 14). Using one of the new, portable hand-held cameras, Lartigue chronicled the use of monied leisure to explore modernity. In formal terms his photographs show a sensitivity to line, a strong contrast of black and white, and an attention to spatial ambiguity, even as they reflect the moods and attitudes of affluent Parisians enjoying the new technology in the years before World War I.

Eugène Atget's thousands of photographs of Paris and its environs constitute an encyclopedic record of a whole environment *en passage.*[6] One of the first large-scale commercial photographers, Atget was an artist of essentially documentary bent, not at all interested in the already-well-established movement of "art photography." Yet his works are compositionally exceptional. Shooting in the Tuileries in 1912, instead of emphasizing the vastness of the gardens he uses overhanging boughs and an allée of trees in the background to close in the space, suggesting a domestic and intimate quality in even this large public park (plate 12). A photograph of a street merchant selling metal baskets (plate 6) likewise conveys the feeling of a living community, if a fading one. Atget gave particular attention to the older buildings of Paris, as in *Residence of the Prince de Condé, rue Monsieur-Le-Prince, 4* (1899–1900; plate 10) and *Cabaret de l'enfer* (1910–11; plate 7). A photograph like *Quai d'Anjou* (1926; plate 11) expresses the mood of this complex period in the city's history, its atmospheric beauty subtly tightened by an undertone of nostalgia and loss.

The replanning of Paris brought wide boulevards on which crowds (and armies) could promenade, broad access to the Seine, the sense of style appropriate to an international metropolis. That artists were fascinated by it is easily understandable. Yet the cost of these alterations, in terms not of money but of human dislocation and worse, brought ambivalence about the advantages of progress. Tens of thousands of people were evicted from their old neighborhoods to make space for the new apartment and office buildings; hand in hand with material improvement came social disruption.

Artists knew this well; in fact the negative effects of industrialization and urbanization were evident to many observers. As a result, visits to the country became a routine of city people both rich and poor. So prevalent were Parisians' "invasions" of once quiet villages in search of clean air, greenery, and respite from the oppressive atmosphere of the city that the word "*villégiature,*" or "resting in the country," took on a new and popular force. Artists too were involved in this social movement; as we shall see in our next chapter, many either moved to or regularly visited suburban or exurban areas in search of relatively unspoiled scenery to make the subject of their work. Although they were stimulated by the confrontation between old and new, and often referred to it, directly or indirectly, in their images, there is a particular note that they often strike: a sense of the countryside as the symbol of a lost world.

4. See Herbert, *Impressionism*, chapter 2, pp. 33–37.

5. See, for example, Naomi Rosenblum, *A World History of Photography* (3rd ed. New York: Abbeville Press, 1997), pp. 278–79, and John Szarkowski and Maria Morris Hambourg, *The Work of Atget*, 4 vols. (New York: The Museum of Modern Art, 1981–85), particularly vol. 2.

6. See Szarkowski and Hambourg, *The Work of Atget.*

PLATE 1. Photographer unknown. ***Panoramic View of Paris (Tuileries Garden)***. c. 1900. Gelatin silver print, 3 1/4 x 11 5/8" (8.3 x 29.6 cm). The Museum of Modern Art, New York. The Family of Man Fund

PLATE 2. Photographer unknown. ***Panoramic View of Paris (Place de la Concorde)***. c. 1900. Gelatin silver print, 3 1/4 x 11 5/8" (8.3 x 29.6 cm). The Museum of Modern Art, New York. The Family of Man Fund

PLATE 3. Photographer unknown.
***Panoramic View of Paris (Place de la
Concorde).*** c. 1900. Gelatin silver print,
3 1/4 x 11 1/2" (8.3 x 29.3 cm). The Museum
of Modern Art, New York. The Family of
Man Fund

PLATE 4. Photographer unknown.
***Panoramic View of Paris (Place de la
Concorde).*** c. 1900. Gelatin silver print,
3 1/4 x 11 9/16" (8.3 x 29.4 cm). The Museum
of Modern Art, New York. The Family of
Man Fund

PLATE 5. Charles Marville. ***Rue du Cygne,
Seen from rue Mondatour.*** c. 1865.
Albumen silver print from a glass
negative, 11 3/4 x 10 9/16" (29.9 x 26.9 cm).
The Museum of Modern Art, New York.
Anonymous Purchase Fund

PLATE 6. Eugène Atget. ***Wire Basket
Peddler (Marchand de paniers de fil de
fer).*** 1899–1900. Albumen silver print,
9 ¹/₄ x 7 ⁷/₈" (23.5 x 18 cm). The Museum
of Modern Art, New York. Abbott-Levy
Collection. Partial gift of Shirley C. Burden

PLATE 7. Eugène Atget. **Cabaret de l'enfer.** 1910–11. Albumen silver print, 8 7/16 x 6 7/8" (21.5 x 17.5 cm). The Museum of Modern Art, New York. Abbott-Levy Collection. Partial gift of Shirley C. Burden

PLATE 8. Edouard-Denis Baldus. **Bibliothèque Impériale, Nouveau Louvre, Paris.** 1856–57. Salt print from a glass negative, 17 7/16 x 13 5/8" (44.4 x 34.9 cm). The Museum of Modern Art, New York. Partial gift of Shirley C. Burden, by exchange

PLATE 9. Edouard-Denis Baldus. ***Church of St. Germain l'Auxerrois.*** c. 1850. Salt print from paper negative, 13 x 17 ¹/₂" (33 x 44.5 cm). The Museum of Modern Art, New York. Purchase

PLATE 10. Eugène Atget. ***Residence of the Prince de Condé, rue Monsieur-Le-Prince, 4.*** 1899–1900. Albumen silver print, 8 ⁹/₁₆ x 7" (21.7 x 18 cm). The Museum of Modern Art, New York. Abbott-Levy Collection. Partial gift of Shirley C. Burden

PLATE 11. Eugène Atget. ***Quai d'Anjou.***
1926. Albumen silver print, 8 9/16 x 7"
(24 x 18 cm). The Museum of Modern
Art, New York. Abbott-Levy Collection.
Partial gift of Shirley C. Burden

PLATE 12. Eugène Atget. *Tuileries,*
Concorde Side (Tuileries, côté Concorde).
1912. Albumen silver print, 6 7/8 x 8 5/8"
(17.5 x 22 cm). The Museum of Modern
Art, New York. Abbott-Levy Collection.
Partial gift of Shirley C. Burden

PLATE 13 (OPPOSITE). Jacques-Henri
Lartigue. **Avenue du Bois de Boulogne,
Paris.** 1910. Gelatin silver print, 15 $^{7}/_{16}$ x
11 $^{11}/_{16}$" (39.2 x 29.7 cm). The Museum of
Modern Art, New York. Gift of the
photographer

PLATE 14. Jacques-Henri Lartigue. **Avenue
du Bois de Boulogne, Paris.** 1911. Gelatin
silver print, 11 $^{5}/_{8}$ x 15 $^{11}/_{16}$" (29.5 x 39.4 cm).
The Museum of Modern Art, New York.
Gift of the photographer

ENVIRONS OF PARIS

As the great metropolis of France, center for every variety of creative and commercial activity, Paris was a magnet for artists from the French provinces and from abroad. Once arrived, however, many of them traveled outside the city to find their pictorial motifs. The towns of the Île-de-France, the region around Paris, were one site of study; another popular place, and one that particularly fascinated Paul Cézanne, was the forest of Fontainebleau.

A generation earlier, Fontainebleau had attracted the painters of the Barbizon School, who began to visit the forest in the 1830s, seeking a local correlative of the types of scenery that had inspired the seventeenth-century Dutch art they so admired. These painters, of whom the most prominent was Théodore Rousseau, considered Fontainebleau an oasis of pure, unspoiled tranquillity (fig. 14); it became a favorite subject of theirs, so much so that the name attached to them, "Barbizon," was the name of a village in the area.[1] These artists relied on close observation, even while they also conveyed a romanticized conception of nature. In fact they presented nature as not only specific but in some way noble, as if it corresponded for them to an ethical category, as well as being beautiful. Their work could be described as "romantic naturalism."

Among the generations that came after the Barbizon School, the Impressionist Claude Monet painted in Fontainebleau in 1863. Cézanne worked there in 1879–80, probably during one of his visits to his friend Emile Zola in Médan. Part of the beauty of the forest comes from the area's geological structure; it is crisscrossed by long narrow ridges, and the woods are scattered with fantastic clusters of rocks. The area shown in *Melting Snow, Fontainebleau* (plate 17) has apparently been quarried since Cézanne visited it, and the spot he saw no longer seems to exist as such; but a photograph found years later among his papers shows a striking resemblance to the scene in his picture (fig. 17). It has been suggested, in fact, that Cézanne was not averse to using a photograph as an aide-mémoire in the studio, and that *Melting Snow, Fontainebleau* was actually painted from the photograph found in his papers.[2]

Recent studies of the locations of Cézanne's paintings, including comparisons with documentary photographs, show how he both responded to

1. See Jean Bouret, *The Barbizon School and 19th Century French Landscape Painting* (Greenwich, Conn.: New York Graphic Society, 1973), and Robert L. Herbert, *Barbizon Revisited*, exh. cat. (New York: Clarke & Way, 1962).

2. This was first suggested by John Rewald, in 1935; see *Les Sites Cézanniens du pays d'Aix: Hommage à John Rewald* (Paris: Réunion des Musées Nationaux et Amis du Musée Granet et de l'oeuvre de Cézanne, 1996), p. 19. See also Pavel Machotka, *Cézanne: Landscape into Art* (New Haven: Yale University Press, 1996), and Van Deren Coke, *The Painter and the Photograph*, exh. cat. (Albuquerque: University of New Mexico Press, 1964), p. 10.

visual structures that effectively already existed in the site and adjusted those structures according to his own vision, his personal perceptual experience, and his attempt to memorialize the "sensation" he felt on studying the motif.[3] His purposes included both fidelity to the subject and respect for the demands of the canvas, and it is this double movement in his work that produces the tension that holds our attention. In *Melting Snow, Fontainebleau*, the general arrangements of the painting and of the photograph coincide, but the painting is enormously intensified by the groupings of short brushstrokes that Cézanne developed in the mid-1870s, the so-called "constructive strokes" that build up forms. The play of light, and the strong sense of pattern, created by these brushstrokes bring the motif to life, and give the work its compositional cohesion. It is interesting to note that *Melting Snow, Fontainebleau* was initially in the collection of Monet; one might wonder whether it was the structure of the light, and its shimmering effects on the snow, that caught the artist's attention.

Cézanne returned to the Fontainebleau forest in the 1890s, and painted, among other works, *Pines and Rocks (Fontainebleau?)* (*Pins et rochers [Fontainebleau?]*) of 1896–99 (plate 18).[4] The composition is firmly structured, its slender verticals—the reddish tree trunks—being rooted in the massive forms of the rocks in the lower part of the picture. The palette is limited to blues, greens, and browns, yet the subtleties of their different shades are full of light. Also bringing light into the picture is the thinness with which Cézanne has applied the paint, giving the work almost the freshness of watercolor. An all-pervading blue tonality envelops the thin soaring trees and shines through the foliage, suggesting the cool, crisp atmosphere of a northern day.

The small towns and villages of the Île-de-France appear in a number of paintings and prints of the period, including Cézanne's *Turning Road at Montgeroult* (*Route tournante à Montgeroult*), from 1898 (plate 24). Montgeroult is a village not far from Pontoise, northeast of Paris. (It is renowned for its château, built in the seventeenth century, during the reign of King Louis XIII, and one of the few surviving examples of the architecture of that period.) Cézanne summered in the village in 1898, and painted two views of it, one of them *Turning Road at Montgeroult*. This is the last fully finished work he executed in the north (all of his important subsequent work is set in Aix). The site of the painting was damaged during World War II, but a photograph taken before the war (fig. 20) suggests that Cézanne followed the local topography in many details, conveying its volumes precisely; he seems, however, to have reordered the foreground, deepening the pictorial space.[5] Leading back into the painting's depth, the road implies compositional recession, which is conveyed, however, not through conventional perspective but through the arrangement of the building forms and masses of foliage. This lush vegetation is rendered as overlapping patches of color, distributed throughout the picture plane and applied in short parallel strokes, forming an almost abstract pattern. We are invited to contemplate a scene caught in its morning beauty—for the color, dominated by strong ochers, cool blues, deep greens, and violets, creates the mood of cool morning air.

The Île-de-France town of Etang-la-Ville, southwest of Paris, is the subject of a group of prints by Ker-Xavier Roussel, a Symbolist painter who was a member of the Nabis (or "Prophets"), an artists' group of the 1890s. *Landscape with Figure Carrying an*

FIGURE 14. Théodore Rousseau. ***Clearing in the Forest of Fontainebleau.*** c. 1860–62. Oil on canvas, 32 ¹/₂ x 57 ¹/₄" (82.5 x 145.4 cm). The Chrysler Museum, Norfolk, Virginia

Umbrella (plate 15) is included in *The Album of Landscapes* (*L'Album de paysage*), a portfolio of lithographs published by the dealer Ambroise Vollard in 1899.[6] Roussel's intimate image is an almost abstract composite of pictorial marks. The umbrella-bearer of the title nearly blends into this rich patterning; the landscape envelops her, a distant woman on the verge of disappearing down a road between meadows and trees. Roussel's style combines the painterly with the graphic, a treatment of trees and foliage that combines the appearance of impasto with a sense that these forms combine in a flat decorative pattern running sinuously throughout the composition. The result is a vibrant scene, in which the strongest presences are the multicolored clumps of foliage—these and the light that shimmers on them, a light also suggested by the large expanses of unprinted white paper, which emphasize the vividness of the lithograph's color.

In August of 1908, after a tense and exhausting winter and a summer illness, Pablo Picasso decided to get out of Paris and went with his mistress Fernande Olivier to La Rue-des-Bois, a village some forty miles north of the city. Within a few days of arriving there Picasso resumed work, completing figures and still lifes but focusing on landscapes, on paper as well as on canvas. This group of works—sometimes referred to as the artist's "green period," because of the prevailing tonality of viridian—evokes the village's calm and tranquil atmosphere.

Although La Rue-des-Bois is near the forest of Halatte, the village itself is set not in woods but in farmland. Yet trees are the predominant motif of the landscapes Picasso painted there. He gave these trees an anthropomorphic quality, and some have seen them as projections of his own vital force; Picasso himself would explain to André Malraux, "I want to see my branches grow....That's why I started to paint trees; yet I never paint them from nature. My trees are myself."[7] This would explain his

3. See Machotka, *Cézanne: Landscape into Art*, p. 138.

4. Until recently this work was dated to 1904, and was believed to show a site in the vicinity of Cézanne's native Aix-en-Provence. It is now thought to have been painted earlier, in Fontainebleau. The reattribution was based on qualities of paint application and brushstroke; in its light, also, the scene seems more northern than Provençal. See William Rubin, ed., *Cézanne. The Late Work*, exh. cat. (New York: The Museum of Modern Art, 1977), cat. 21, p. 392.

5. See ibid., cat. 19, p. 391, and Machotka, *Cézanne: Landscape into Art*, pp. 94–96, 138.

6. See *Edouard Vuillard à K.-X Roussel*, exh. cat. (Paris: Orangerie des Tuileries, 1968).

FIGURE 15. Henri Rousseau. *The Snake Charmer.*
1907. Oil on canvas, 66 1/2 x 74 1/2" (169 x 189.5 cm).
Musée du Louvre, Paris

indifference to the backwater farmland around La Rue-des-Bois, where, according to Olivier, the living conditions were quite primitive. She later remembered, "We had to live pretty much as if we were camping, but Pablo enjoyed the peace and tranquillity, although he didn't like the scenery. The surrounding forest was magnificent, but I realized that Picasso felt quite out of place in the French countryside. He found it too damp and monotonous....He preferred the...warm odors of the rosemary, thyme, and cypress of his native land."[8] Clearly Picasso's landscapes from La Rue-des-Bois were more conceptual than descriptive. They had little to do with the local landscape even of the forest of Halatte, for they conveyed, not the nature the artist saw, but his feelings about nature, the emotion and vision he projected onto it.

Another important aspect of Picasso's landscapes at La Rue-des-Bois is the fact that he did not make the scenery a backdrop for figures, but focused narrowly on elements of the landscape itself, as if rethinking the concepts and conventions of Henri Rousseau and of Cézanne. The work of Rousseau, which Picasso had known for nearly a decade,[9] had shown him examples of the visual potential of simplified form, pictorial flatness (through a compression of perspectival depth), and a certain quality of awkwardness. Rousseau's monumental painting *The Snake Charmer* (1907; fig. 15), exhibited at the 1907 Salon d'automne in Paris, was a particular influence on Picasso's "green period" manner of depicting natural forms as simple, schematic, stylized, and relatively lacking in detail.

That summer of 1908, Picasso also seems to have been thinking about Cézanne's emphasis on pictorial structure, his technique of building an image out of small brushstrokes, his rejection of a single viewpoint, his manipulation of traditional perspective, and his achievement of a sculptural, relief effect through an interplay of light and shade. Picasso also makes creative use of Cézanne's device of *passage*, creating open shapes that bleed into one another, even when the objects described are on different visual planes. In *Landscape* (plate 23), which combines the influences of both of the older artists, Picasso limits his palette to darker and lighter greens, with touches of yellow and brown; the landscape is airless, stressing not space but mass. There is also an ambivalence as to whether the space is moving forward or receding. The approach was new for Picasso, and shortly after his return from La Rue-des-Bois, three of the works he had executed there, including *Landscape*, were acquired by Gertrude Stein and her brother Leo Stein, famous collectors of avant-garde art. Works like this one eventually led Picasso toward the invention of the new modernist language that took Cézanne's formal inventions one step further—toward Cubism.[10]

The native French landscape fascinated photographers as well as painters. As early as the 1850s—less than twenty years after the medium's invention, and at a time when photographic equipment was still heavy and unwieldy—Eugène Cuvelier was working outdoors in the forest of Fontainebleau, following on the heels of the Barbizon School. Later in the century and in the first part of the next, Eugène Atget took thousands of photographs communicating the myriad moods not only of Paris but of the countryside around it (plates 16, 20, 22, 25–27).

As a medium, photography allowed artists to capture both the enduring topographical specificity of a particular site and its evanescent quality at any one moment—the mood, the light, at a particular fragment of a second on a particular day. Thus Taupin's *Nature Study* (c. 1865–75; plate 19) portrays not only a picturesque copse around a pond but the fleeting reflections of the trees in the water. The same device appears in many canvases by Monet, particularly in his Poplar series of 1888–91 (plate 29), and he and the other Impressionists put a high value on immediacy of response and sensitivity to the flux of appearances; but in photography the sense of the irrecoverable instant is still more acute. At the same time, views of Fontainebleau by Cuvelier (plate 21) and Atget (plate 22) record the spirit of peace and mystery that Cézanne, too, seems to have found in the forest—and these two photographers themselves were working some sixty years apart (Cuvelier in the 1850s). All of these artists, whatever their medium of expression, responded in some way to the region around Paris, and found qualities in it that they tried to reveal through their work. In admiring the work, we are inspired to appreciate the landscape that served as its model.

7. Pablo Picasso, quoted in André Malraux, *Picasso's Mask*, trans. June Guicharnaud with Jacques Guicharnaud (New York: Da Capo Press, 1994), p. 137. See also John Richardson, *The Painter of Modern Life*, vol. 2 of *A Life of Picasso* (New York: Random House, 1996), pp. 93–99.

8. Fernande Olivier, quoted in Richardson, *The Painter of Modern Life*, p. 94. See also Olivier, *Souvenirs intimes*, ed. Gilbert Krill (Paris: Calmann-Lévy, 1988).

9. See Richardson, *The Painter of Modern Life*, p. 93; Kirk Varnedoe, *Masterpieces from the David and Peggy Rockefeller Collection: Manet to Picasso*, exh. cat. (New York: The Museum of Modern Art, 1994), p. 58; and Rubin et al., *Picasso in the Collection of The Museum of Modern Art* (New York: The Museum of Modern Art, 1972), p. 51.

10. See Rubin, "Cézannisme and the Beginnings of Cubism," in Rubin, ed., *Cézanne: The Late Work*, pp. 151–202, and Maria Teresa Ocaña et al., *Picasso: Landscapes 1890–1912* (Barcelona: Museu Picasso, 1994).

PLATE 15. Ker-Xavier Roussel. ***Landscape with Figure Carrying an Umbrella*** from the portfolio ***The Album of Landscapes (L'Album de paysage).*** 1899. Lithograph, comp: 9 $^1/_4$ x 14" (23.5 x 35.6 cm). The Museum of Modern Art, New York. Gift of Hubert de Givenchy

FIGURE 16. Etang-la-Ville, n.d. Postcard

PLATE 16. Eugène Atget. *Saint-Cloud.*
1915–19. Albumen silver print, 6 $^7/_8$ x 9 $^1/_{16}$"
(17.5 x 23 cm). The Museum of Modern Art,
New York. Abbott-Levy Collection. Partial
gift of Shirley C. Burden

PLATE 17. Paul Cézanne. **Melting Snow, Fontainebleau.** c. 1879–80. Oil on canvas, 29 x 39 ⁵/₈" (73.5 x 100.7 cm). The Museum of Modern Art, New York. Gift of André Meyer

FIGURE 17. Photograph resembling the site of **Melting Snow, Fontainebleau**, found among Cézanne's papers. n.d.

PLATE 18. Paul Cézanne. ***Pines and Rocks (Fontainebleau?) (Pins et rochers [Fontainebleau?]).*** 1896–99. Oil on canvas, 32 x 25³/₄" (81.3 x 65.4 cm). The Museum of Modern Art, New York. Lillie P. Bliss Collection

FIGURE 18. Georges Balagny. ***Scotch Fir, Path, Rocks.*** 1877. Albumen silver print, 11³/₄ x 10¹/₄" (29.8 x 25.9 cm). Département des Estampes et de la Photographie, Bibliothèque Nationale de France, Paris

PLATE 19 (OPPOSITE). Taupin. **Nature Study.** c. 1865–75. Albumen silver print from a glass negative, 10 1/2 x 8 3/8" (26.7 x 21.3 cm). The Museum of Modern Art, New York. John Parkinson III Fund

PLATE 20. Eugène Atget. **Forest, Fontainebleau (Forêt, Fontainebleau).** 1925. Albumen silver print by Richard Benson from the original negative, 7 x 9 9/16" (18 x 24.3 cm). The Museum of Modern Art, New York. Abbott-Levy Collection. Partial gift of Shirley C. Burden

PLATE 21 (LEFT). Eugène Cuvelier. ***By the Bodmer Oak Tree, Forest of Fontainebleau.*** Late 1850s. Albumen silver print from a paper negative, 13 5/8 x 10" (34.6 x 25.5 cm). The Museum of Modern Art, New York. Joel and Anne Ehrenkranz Fund

PLATE 22 (ABOVE). Eugène Atget. ***Beech Tree (Le Hêtre).*** 1910–15. Albumen silver print, 8 1/2 x 6 3/4" (21.6 x 17.1 cm). The Museum of Modern Art, New York. Given anonymously

PLATE 23. Pablo Picasso. *Landscape.* 1908.
Oil on canvas, 39 5/8 x 32" (100.8 x 81.3 cm).
The Museum of Modern Art, New York.
Gift of Mr. and Mrs. David Rockefeller

FIGURE 19. Village street, La Rue-des-Bois,
n.d. Postcard

PLATE 24. Paul Cézanne. ***Turning Road at Montgeroult (Route tournante à Montgeroult).*** 1898. Oil on canvas, 32 x 25 7/8" (81.3 x 65.7 cm). The Museum of Modern Art, New York. Mrs. John Hay Whitney Bequest

FIGURE 20. Montgeroult, Val d'Oise, c. 1935. John Rewald Library Collection, Archives of the National Gallery of Art, Washington, D.C.

PLATE 25. Eugène Atget. *Abbeville (Lane)*
(Abbeville [Chemin]). Before 1900.
Albumen silver print, 6 ¹¹/₁₆ x 9 ¹/₁₆"
(17 x 23 cm). The Museum of Modern Art,
New York. Abbott-Levy Collection. Partial
gift of Shirley C. Burden

PLATE 26. Eugène Atget. *Abbeville (Somme).* Before 1900. Albumen silver print, 6 ¹¹/₁₆ x 8 ¹⁵/₁₆" (17 x 22.7 cm). The Museum of Modern Art, New York. Abbott-Levy Collection. Partial gift of Shirley C. Burden

PLATE 27. Eugène Atget. ***Entrance to the Gardens (Entrée des jardins).*** 1921–22. Albumen silver print, 8 $^{7}/_{16}$ x 6 $^{7}/_{8}$" (22.7 x 17 cm). The Museum of Modern Art, New York. Abbott-Levy Collection. Partial gift of Shirley C. Burden

NORMANDY, THE CHANNEL, AND BRITTANY

Outside the immediate environs of Paris, one of the first regions to be explored by the landscape artists of the later nineteenth century was Normandy, in northwestern France, a region of coast and sea.

Nor were artists the only visitors; the growth of the railways and the improvement of roads had opened the way for the region to become an affluent summer resort area. In fact an entire leisure industry was developing there: hotels, restaurants, casinos. The bourgeois families of the cities, initiating the organized activity of vacationing as we know it today, went to Normandy to see the places they had read about in the period's proliferation of travel books and magazines. Small port towns like Honfleur, and fishing villages like Pourville, began to attract temporary summer populations, everyone seeking a little solitude, a little respite from their effacement in the urban crowd, but everyone ending up participating in what has been called a "collective gaze"—a collective viewing of all the same sites that the community as a body had decided should be seen.[1]

Among the visitors, the more affluent, able to take prolonged vacations, might spend a summer in a rented villa or a luxurious hotel, enjoying the pleasures of leisure in an increasingly fashionable place that everyone agreed was picturesque. Working-class folk would come for shorter stays, but they too would enjoy the countryside and beaches. The virtues of preindustrial, premodern landscapes were increasingly widely advertised, and the new ease of travel made them ever more accessible.

The Impressionist painter Claude Monet grew up in the Norman port of Le Havre, and considered himself native to the region. Later, after he moved to Paris, he took many of his vacations in Normandy, and beginning in 1862, he often painted there, working with his mentors Eugène Boudin and Johann Barthold Jongkind (figs. 21 and 22).[2] As subjects Monet chose both destinations familiar to any summer visitor (Honfleur, Trouville, Pourville) and quieter villages and hamlets. In his work in the tourist spots, he often picked the predictable subjects and views, which tended, after all, to honor the defining characterics of the place; yet he preferred to avoid depicting tourists and their activities, or for that matter any sign of "contamination" by tourism (though he was not averse to participating in such activities himself). Generally painting landscapes that offered little trace of modernity, he,

1. See Robert L. Herbert, *Monet on the Normandy Coast: Tourism and Painting, 1867–1886* (New Haven and London: Yale University Press, 1994), pp. 4–5, and John Urry, *The Tourist Gaze: Leisure and Travel in Contemporary Societies* (New Haven and London: Yale University Press, 1990).

2. See Herbert, *Monet on the Normandy Coast.*

FIGURE 21. Eugène Boudin. **Coast of Brittany.** 1870. Oil on canvas, 18 5/8 x 26" (47.3 x 66 cm). National Gallery of Art, Washington, D.C. Collection of Mr. and Mrs. Paul Mellon

like the travelers of the preindustrial period, was a participant in what has been described as a "romantic gaze," as opposed to the tourists' "collective gaze."[3] But although there were differences of selectivity and sophistication, there was also a great deal of traffic and commonality between these two kinds of visual habit, for the collective gaze was much informed by a romantic understanding of landscape—and also, eventually, by paintings like Monet's. And if Monet sought out the less touristic views (sometimes, in his paintings, removing traces of tourism from scenes in which they were present), he was only doing what all tourists do, or wish they could.

Monet's romantic heritage appears clearly in *On the Cliff at Pourville, Clear Weather* (plate 28), painted in 1882.[4] Here Monet takes a seagull's-eye view, a vertiginous aerial suspension high above the water. The dizzying height, the dramatic confrontation of cliffs and sea, the sense of nature's size—all this recalls the art of the romantic sublime that had emerged roughly a century earlier, for example the work of Caspar David Friedrich. At the same time, the work is domestic and familiar: where Friedrich's mountaintops are mystically remote, Monet's viewpoint—that of a solitary stroller, surveying the English Channel from above—must have been accessible to any visitor to Pourville, an unpretentious small port two or three miles west of Dieppe. Also, the many diminutive sailboats relate the picture to the leisure activities of summer vacationers, a subject Friedrich would never have addressed.

The year before, on the Norman coast at Fécamp, Monet had executed a number of seascapes, and sixteen of these had quickly sold. Encouraged by this success, Monet stayed at Pourville from early February through April of 1882 and then again from mid-June until early October, painting some ninety seascapes and a dozen other works. (One of these, *The Cliffs at Pourville*, in the Nationalmuseum in Stockholm, strongly resembles *On the Cliff at Pourville* in both its composition and its vantage point.) In all of the pictures of this period, Monet uses a forceful technique and vigorous brushwork, vividly evoking dramatic waves, jagged rocks in the surf, and other natural elements. In earlier periods his brushwork had been more delicate; here, though, the surfaces of the paintings are densely built up. In his treatment of shapes, colors, and shadows, he also emphasizes the effect of bright light. The sharply dropping viewpoint in *On the Cliff at Pourville* reveals

FIGURE 22. Johan-Barthold Jongkind. **Ruins of the Château of Rosemont.** 1861. Oil on canvas, 13 1/4 x 22 1/4" (34 x 56.5 cm). Musée d'Orsay, Paris

the influence of Japanese woodblock prints (fig. 23), which Monet avidly collected and admired.[5] Like a number of other artists of the period, including Paul Gauguin and Vincent van Gogh, he also applied the compositional devices of those prints in his own work.

In 1883, Monet settled in the old Norman hamlet of Giverny, in a pink stucco house that he first rented, then bought.[6] The gardens of this house are immortalized in the many pictures he painted of them over the next forty years, indeed almost until his death, in 1926. Giverny stands in a triangle of land formed by the meeting of the Epte and the Seine, and these rivers, along with the pond he created in his garden, gave Monet enormous opportu-

FIGURE 23. Katsushika Hokusai. *The Great Wave of Kanagawa,* from the series *Thirty-Six Views of Mount Fuji.* 1831. Woodblock print, 9 7/8 x 14 5/8" (25 x 37.1 cm). Victoria and Albert Museum, London

nities to explore the different qualities of light as it is reflected off water. His interest in light as the determining factor in a viewer's sense of a place led him to many studies of the same motif at different times of the day and in different weathers; and after 1888 he produced a number of a series based on this principle—the Haystacks of 1888–91, followed by Poplars (1888–91), Rouen Cathedral (1892–95), and Morning on the Seine (1896–97).

Poplars at Giverny, Sunrise (1888; plate 29) presents a favorite motif of Monet's: the bright rising sun illuminating a group of poplar trees. The linear arrangement of the composition recalls paintings by the seventeenth-century Dutch master Meindert Hobbema (fig. 6). For each painting in the Poplars series, it is believed, Monet initially worked outdoors, and very quickly, trying to capture the fleeting moment. He would then bring the canvas into the studio for an often protracted second campaign, moving the image toward chromatic harmony by working and reworking the surface until he had built up a thick layer of paint. In treating a single motif in an enormous variety of ways depending on the response of his eye to the light, Monet's serial works clearly reveal his astonishing inventiveness. The patterns of his brushstrokes simultaneously evoke flatness and volume; an almost abstract web of marks is also a clear description, of delicate leaves shimmering in the morning light as a mosaic of yellows, blues, greens, and purples.

For the last three decades of his life, Monet focused his painting on his beloved Giverny garden, which he was continuously improving and beautifying. In the spring of 1893, ten years after settling in Giverny, he decided to construct a pond by diverting water from the nearby Epte; completed by the autumn of that year, the pond was later enlarged, in 1901, 1903, and 1910 (figs. 28, 29). The water was filled with water lilies and surrounded by flowers, shrubs, and trees. Crossing over it was a Japanese-type bridge, initially simple, later embellished with an arbor or trellis. We have already seen Monet's interest in Japanese aesthetics revealed in the deep, oblique perspective of view in *On the Cliff at Pourville,* and his Giverny

3. See ibid., p. 46, and Urry, *The Tourist Gaze,* p. 97 ff.

4. On Monet at Pourville see Herbert, *Monet on the Normandy Coast,* pp. 37–49.

5. See Colta Feller Ives, *The Great Wave: The Influence of Japanese Woodcuts on French Prints* (New York: The Metropolitan Museum of Art, 1974).

6. On Monet at Giverny see *Monet's Years at Giverny: Beyond Impressionism,* exh. cat. (New York: The Metropolitan Museum of Art, 1978), and Lynne Federle Orr, *Monet: Late Painting of Giverny from the Musée Marmottan* (New York: Harry N. Abrams, 1994).

garden included not only the Japanese bridge but Japanese plantings: ginkgos, bamboos, oriental fruit trees.

In 1899, Monet began a series of paintings of the Japanese bridge—eighteen works altogether, showing the structure from different angles and in different lights. Many photographs allow us to compare the actual appearance of the bridge at various moments with his depictions of it. *The Japanese Footbridge* of c. 1920–22 (plate 30) shows the bridge after the addition of the arbor, creating a canopy of wisteria blooms visible in figure 28. A thick web of multicolored brushstrokes—an almost abstract pattern of pictorial marks, applied in a heavy impasto to create a dense material surface—reflects the profusion of foliage. The rusts and oranges accompanying the green in the palette suggest the work was painted in the fall.

Similar effects of thick, crusty, bright-colored surface appear in another of Monet's late works, *Agapanthus* (c. 1918–25; plate 31), one of his several paintings of this particular plant, some of them combining it with water lilies. The blossoms of agapanthus can be lilac or white in color; from descriptions and photographs of Monet's garden, we know that it was white agapanthus he planted around the edge of the pond, along with purple iris. In this painting the plant's feathery blooms take on a lavender tone, probably a result of the optical mixture of purple and white, viewed against the greens of the foliage. An impassioned colorist, Monet experimented constantly with light, color, and texture, trying to convey the multitude of nature's nuances that he saw in the orchestrated color environment that was his garden.

The generation that followed after Monet and the Impressionists drew no less pleasure from the ports and villages of Normandy; Georges Seurat passed a number of summers there, beginning in 1885, when he was in his mid-twenties. That year, during a stay in Grandcamp, Seurat undertook several paintings of marine subjects. These works extended the seascape tradition that had originated with Claude-Joseph Vernet, in the eighteenth century (fig. 24), and had been continued earlier in the nineteenth century by the Le Havre artist Boudin (fig. 21), the Dutch-born landscape artist Jongkind (fig. 22), and the Barbizon School painter Charles-François Daubigny (fig. 25—all three of these artists, incidentally, had been mentors for Monet). Seurat's marines represented an expansion of his themes—his previous works had been landscapes, figure compositions, and scenes of urban life—and reflected his enthusiasm for Impressionism. His interest in coastal views was furthered by his family's observance of the newly developed bourgeois practice of vacationing in such places as Normandy and the Channel coast.

Right from the start, it would seem, Normandy's misty northern light, to Seurat's

FIGURE 24. Joseph Vernet. *A Sea-Shore.* 1776. Oil on copper, 24 1/2 x 33 1/2" (62.2 x 85.1 cm). National Gallery, London

eye, gave color a moody quality, a certain luminous stillness. Where Monet's seascapes show nature as majestic and vibrantly alive, Seurat's *English Channel at Grandcamp* (*La Manche à Grandcamp*; plate 35), painted that first summer there, emanates stillness and quiet. Grandcamp was a port, and there are boats in view, but even so the place seems devoid of human presence or activity. The composition is formally quite traditional, with the bushes in the foreground serving as a *repoussoir* device to give

FIGURE 25. Charles-François Daubigny. *Villerville-sur-Mer.* 1864 and 1874. Oil on canvas, 39 3/8 x 78 3/4" (100 x 200 cm). H. W. Mesdag Museum, The Hague

the picture depth, but the work is updated by its brush technique and by its color. Using a system based on the theories of Eugène Chevreul and Ogden Rood,[7] and a palette of pure and earth colors derived from Eugène Delacroix,[8] Seurat would apply paint as separate, adjoining touches of prismatic hues, placed so that contrasting complementaries would optically mix in the viewer's eye. The technique—called pointillist, for its small dotlike brush marks, or divisionist, for its division of color into constituent tones—was intended to create luminosity and coloristic harmony.

The following year—1886—Seurat summered in Honfleur between June and mid-August, producing seven canvases there. One of these is *Evening, Honfleur* (plate 33), a sunset view of the Seine estuary, and perhaps a nocturnal pendant to another work, *The Shore at Bas-Butin, Honfleur,* which was painted in the same area (on the west edge of the town, beyond the harbor, and a short distance from where Seurat was staying) but looking in the opposite direction, and in broad daylight. A serene vision of the site, *Evening, Honfleur* is dominated by a high, light-filled expanse of sky, rendered with small strokes of color and structured horizontally by the long thin bars of blue clouds. This upward-lifting ethereal plane acts as a counterweight to the lower part of the canvas, where a triangular section of beach is sharply cut by the dark diagonals of the breakwaters. The careful use of different-sized brushstrokes—a ground layer of larger strokes overlaid with a layer of smaller ones (the smallest possibly added three or four years later)—tightens the surface. Seurat had also begun the practice of placing the smallest strokes in the very center of larger ones, a technique he would apply more extensively in works of the summer of 1888 such as *Port-en-Bessin, Entrance to the Harbor* (plate 34). An important feature of the painting is the wide painted frame, which Seurat added in 1889 or 1890, following a popular practice of the Symbolist artists.[9] The frame extends the pictorial field out beyond the edges of the canvas, and gives it a three-dimensional depth. Here the painting's basic colors are intermixed in different intensities, restating the work's palette and mood in another register.

Seurat did not go to Normandy in 1887, but spent the summer of 1888 in Port-en-Bessin, a fishing village some fifteen miles west of Grandcamp

7. See John Rewald, *Post-Impressionism: From van Gogh to Gauguin* (3rd ed. New York: The Museum of Modern Art, 1978), p. 73 ff.

8. On Georges Seurat and Delacroix, see ibid., p. 73. Signac wrote a thesis, *D'Eugène Delacroix au Neo-Impressionisme* (1899), on Delacroix and Neo-Impressionism; see Linda Nochlin, *Impressionism and Post-Impressionism, 1874–1900* (Englewood Cliffs, N.J.: Prentice Hall, 1966), pp. 116–23.

9. See Herbert, "Seurat's Painted Borders and Frames," in Herbert, with Françoise Cachin et al., *Georges Seurat, 1859–1891,* exh. cat. (New York: The Metropolitan Museum of Art, 1991), p. 376.

and very much in the same spirit. Chalk cliffs and granite breakwaters are characteristic elements of the landscape. Here Seurat began six paintings (some of them may have been finished later), including *Port-en-Bessin, Entrance to the Harbor*. He established the group conceptually much as he had in his paintings of Honfleur two years earlier, showing the sea at different times of the day and at different tides.

Port-en-Bessin is a coastal Norman village with Roman ruins, but Seurat ignored its tourist attractions in favor of the working port, where boats filled a harbor between stone jetties. Once again, however, he eliminated any sign of workplace bustle, and in fact any human figure. Many of the paintings and drawings he produced in Paris show figures in all kinds of activities, but when he came to Normandy he made his focus the sea. *Port-en-Bessin, Entrance to the Harbor* does show sailboats, and these vessels for the pleasure of vacationers are depicted in shimmering sunlight, their white sails playing joyfully against the blues and greens of the water and the ochers of the jetties and of the patches of sand on the shore. A view of Port-en-Bessin from above (fig. 32) suggests that the artist may have stood on one of the cliffs above the village, looking down at it, but decided to omit all sign of its architecture excepting the ends of the two jetties. Like *Evening, Honfleur*, the work has a frame painted by the artist; the colors are related to those in the painting, but have a darker tonality, a contrast that has the effect of making the painting look brighter. The overall mood is that of a peaceful summer day. Light clouds in the sky are reflected in the water as patches of darker blue. In its formal structure the composition has been compared to a sequence of musical movements resulting in a contrapuntal whole.[10]

In the summer of 1890 Seurat stayed in Gravelines, a small French port not in Normandy proper but northeast of it, near the Belgian border. Here he produced his last four seascapes.[11] (He died in the spring of the following year.) Gravelines is in Flanders, the flat country around Calais and running north into Belgium. Where Norman port towns are often dominated by steep bluffs and cliffs, Gravelines lies in a large coastal plain, with low dunes along the sea. The village itself—which is slightly inland, and boasts a hexagonal seventeenth-century fortress—held no interest for Seurat, at least not as a subject for painting; he chose instead two hamlets a little downstream, Petit-Fort-Philippe and Grand-Fort-Philippe, on either side of the river Aa. The works he painted here, sometimes called the "Gravelines Quartet," are today dispersed among four different collections; it is *The Channel at Gravelines, Evening* (plate 32) that is in the collection of The Museum of Modern Art.

Seurat's works of that season are more austere, more static, than his earlier marines. Not only does he reduce human activity and show no human figures, as was his habit in these scenes, he also makes *The Channel at Gravelines* strikingly frontal and rectilinear—it could almost be charted on a graph. Although Seurat certainly based the painting on what he saw as he stood on the quay in Petit-Fort-Philippe (fig. 30), he was not an adherent of the Impressionist principle of reacting quickly and spontaneously to nature, and he planned his works carefully and methodically. (Before painting *The Channel at Gravelines*, he produced a body of preparatory pictures, including an oil sketch and four conté-crayon drawings.) Here he gives the quay in the foreground a slight curve to provide some indication of depth, but otherwise makes the picture largely a series of bars and planes. That gentle curve of the quay, and the curves of the boats' sails, temper the geometry of the picture's other components, all verticals, horizontals, and diagonals playing against each other tautly but harmoniously.

The Channel at Gravelines was the last canvas Seurat painted that summer—the final chord of the quartet. It is harsher in color than the other three works in the group, which are pearlier in tone. The scene is remarkably still, a suspended moment, and its atmosphere is serene, perhaps even remote—but then Seurat's rational, scientific manner of applying color, in small, carefully organized brushstrokes of different sizes, often gives his work a certain formality. The picture nevertheless has a contemplative quality that is strong and compelling. In choosing an evening light for the picture, Seurat follows the Impressionist practice (particularly Monet's) of turning effects of atmosphere into effects of artistic expression.

Seurat's younger friend and disciple Paul Signac was another Neo-Impressionist artist who used the pointillist brushstroke to examine the sites of Normandy. (He was influenced in his technique by both Seurat and the older Impressionist Camille Pissarro.) In 1895, Signac visited the Norman village of Les Andelys—in a sense the birthplace of the classical tradition of French landscape painting, for Nicolas Poussin was born nearby, in 1594. Signac's lithograph *Les Andelys* (plate 38) extolls the rustic beauty of Les Andelys, with its domestic architecture, thatched roofs, and riverside location. Where an Impressionist painter would have used spontaneous brushwork to try to catch the light and weather of a moment, Signac applies color deliberately and stresses the quiet stability of the scene. Although modified by human presence, nature here is harmonious and tranquil, untouched by modernity, industrialization, or tourism.

BRITTANY

More unspoiled still, in fact a backwater of the French countryside, was Brittany, with its rugged Atlantic coastline to the south and west of Normandy. Beginning in the 1860s, two Breton towns in particular, Pont-Aven and Le Pouldu, began to attract artists. Pont-Aven lies some ten miles inland, on the Aven river; the smaller village of Le Pouldu is a dozen miles away, at the mouth of the Laita river, on a rocky coast here and there punctuated by sandy beaches. In 1864, an American called Henri Bacon, joined by his compatriots Robert Wylie and Charles G. Way, founded a colony of American artists in Pont-Aven, and the town shortly became a meeting place for artists trying to live cheaply in picturesque surroundings.

In the main square of Pont-Aven were three hotels, one of them the now-famous *pension* of Marie-Jeanne Gloanec. Here, in July of 1886, Paul Gauguin installed himself for a six-month stay, returning for several months more in 1888. From then until 1891, when he decided to leave France for the South Seas, he would visit Brittany regularly, and by 1893 he and his friends Emile Bernard, Charles Laval, and Paul Sérusier, among others, had become known as the School of Pont-Aven—although the honor would more appropriately have gone to Le Pouldu. For although it was at Pont-Aven that Gauguin's work started to

10. See ibid., cat. 207, p. 329.

11. See Ellen Wardwell Lee, *Seurat at Gravelines: The Last Landscapes*, exh. cat. (Indianapolis: Indianapolis Museum of Art, in collaboration with Indiana University Press, 1990).

attract attention, it was at Le Pouldu, where the artist began to stay after 1889, that he and the Symbolist (or Synthetist) artists around him created their most important works, a principal stylistic characteristic being the use of large areas of flat, unmodulated color contained within sinuous contours.

Among the attractions of Brittany for artists, certainly, was the fact that it was an inexpensive place to live. (Normandy, by contrast, was far more bourgeois, and more financially demanding.) But Gauguin and the others were above all attracted to Brittany because it seemed to them wild and remote, its culture archaic, apparently far removed from industrialization, urbanization, and modernity. In a letter to his friend Emile Schuffenecker in February 1888, Gauguin wrote, "I love Brittany. I find wildness and primitiveness there. When my wooden shoes ring on this granite, I hear the muffled, dull, and powerful tone which I try to achieve in painting."[12]

Le Pouldu was a particularly seductive place. It was quieter than Pont-Aven, the climate was mild, and the village was a delight—a scattered group of relatively isolated farmhouses, set among softly rolling fields and hills speckled with flowering fig and almond trees (fig. 35). This is the scenery that Sérusier described in his lithograph *The Soil of Brittany* (*La Terre bretonne*), of 1892–93 (plate 39). Executed in the Synthetist idiom, with heavy contours delineating the shapes of the hills, the work is typical of Sérusier's landscapes of the period. It is organized in almost horizontal bands—foreground, middle ground, sky. The tiny figures of Breton peasants blend into the landscape, their rounded outlines reflecting the larger forms of the rocks; this unity of landscape and figure reflects Sérusier's philosophical and spiritual interests, for he was a firm believer in the harmonious unity of the peasant and his or her environment. As a Theosophist, like many of his fellow Symbolists, Sérusier was preoccupied with the interrelationships of living and nonliving things, and of inner truths and outer appearances, and tried to convey these ideas in his art. The Breton peasantry, with their deep attachment to their land, seemed the perfect subject through which to suggest such principles. In its charm and force, the landscape of Brittany proved a resource for many artists seeking imagery expressive of their Symbolist and spiritual concerns.

12. Paul Gauguin, letter to Emile Schuffenecker, February 1888, in *Gauguin et l'Ecole de Pont-Aven*, exh. cat. (Paris: Bibliothèque Nationale, 1989), p. 6. Quoted here as trans. from the French in Rewald, *Post-Impressionism: From van Gogh to Gauguin*, p. 171.

PLATE 28. Claude Monet. ***On the Cliff at Pourville, Clear Weather.*** 1882. Oil on canvas, 25 1/2 x 31 3/4" (64.7 x 80.7 cm). The Museum of Modern Art, New York. Fractional gift of Janice H. Levin

FIGURE 26. Town and cliffs of Pourville, n.d. Postcard

PLATE 29. Claude Monet. ***Poplars at Giverny, Sunrise.*** 1888. Oil on canvas, 29$^{1}/_{8}$ x 36$^{1}/_{2}$" (74 x 92.7 cm). The Museum of Modern Art, New York. The William B. Jaffe and Evelyn A. J. Hall Collection

FIGURE 27. Meadows along the River Epte, Giverny, n.d. Postcard

PLATE 30. Claude Monet. *The Japanese Footbridge.* c. 1920–22. Oil on canvas, 35 1/4 x 45 7/8" (89.5 x 116.3 cm). The Museum of Modern Art, New York. Grace Rainey Rogers Fund

FIGURE 28. The Japanese footbridge in Monet's garden, Giverny, 1924. Photograph: Georges Truffaut

PLATE 31. Claude Monet. **Agapanthus.**
c. 1918–25. Oil on canvas, 6' 6" x 70 1/4"
(198.2 x 178.4 cm). The Museum of
Modern Art, New York. Gift of Sylvia
Slifka in memory of Joseph Slifka

FIGURE 29. The water-lily pond in Monet's
garden, Giverny, 1933

PLATE 32. Georges-Pierre Seurat. *The Channel at Gravelines, Evening.* 1890. Oil on canvas, 25³/₄ x 32¹/₄" (65.4 x 81.9 cm). The Museum of Modern Art, New York. Gift of Mr. and Mrs. William A. M. Burden

FIGURE 30. The quay at Petit-Fort-Philippe, Gravelines, n.d. Postcard

PLATE 33. Georges-Pierre Seurat. *Evening, Honfleur.* 1886. Oil on canvas, 25 3/4 x 32" (65.4 x 81.1 cm). The Museum of Modern Art, New York. Gift of Mrs. David M. Levy

FIGURE 31. Honfleur from the air, n.d. Postcard

PLATE 34. Georges-Pierre Seurat. ***Port-en-Bessin, Entrance to the Harbor.*** 1888. Oil on canvas, 21⅝ x 25⅝" (54.9 x 65.1 cm). The Museum of Modern Art, New York. Lillie P. Bliss Collection

FIGURE 32. Town and cliffs of Port-en-Bessin, n.d. Postcard

PLATE 35. Georges-Pierre Seurat.
***The English Channel at Grandcamp
(La Manche à Grandcamp).*** 1885. Oil
on canvas, 26 x 32 ¹/₂" (66.2 x 82.4 cm).
The Museum of Modern Art, New York.
Estate of John Hay Whitney

FIGURE 33. Fishermen's boats at
Grandcamp, n.d. Postcard

PLATE 36. Jacques-Henri Lartigue. *The Beach at Villerville.* 1908. Gelatin silver print, 10¹/₂ x 13¹/₄" (26.7 x 33.6 cm). The Museum of Modern Art, New York. Purchase

PLATE 37. Eugène Atget. *La Rochelle.*
1896? Albumen silver print, 6 5/8 x 8 13/16"
(16 x 20.8 cm). The Museum of Modern
Art, New York. Abbott-Levy Collection.
Partial gift of Shirley C. Burden

PLATE 38. Paul Signac. ***Les Andelys.*** 1895.
Lithograph, comp: 12 x 18" (30.5 x 45.8 cm).
The Museum of Modern Art, New York.
Abby Aldrich Rockefeller Fund

FIGURE 34. Les Andelys, n.d. Postcard

PLATE 39. Paul Sérusier. **The Soil of Brittany (La Terre bretonne)** from the album **L'Epreuve.** 1895. Lithograph, comp: 9 3/8 x 8 5/8" (23.8 x 21.9 cm). The Museum of Modern Art, New York. Abby Aldrich Rockefeller Fund

FIGURE 35. Le Pouldu, n.d. Postcard

BURGUNDY, OR THE CÔTE D'OR

It may seem a contradiction that the French landscape artists of the later nineteenth century spent so much time in Paris, some putting in years there before moving elsewhere, some visiting regularly and for long periods, many living there permanently. But it was the quality of modern urban life, surely, a quality then new and emergent, that focused their interest on rural environments, and meanwhile the growing ease of travel made it possible for them both to benefit from the intellectual and professional advantages of the metropolitan existence and to travel regularly to other parts of the country. Travel was their inspiration and stimulant, and they wandered not only to the fashionable coastal resorts of the English Channel and the wilder shores of Brittany but to less obviously scenic places such as the farmland and vineyards of Burgundy, or the Côte d'Or.

Two exquisite monotypes by Edgar Degas, *Green Landscape* (*Paysage vert*; plate 40) and *A Wooded Landscape* (*Forêt dans la montagne*; plate 41), show the landscapes that Degas discovered on a journey through Burgundy in September of 1890. Traveling in a two-wheeled horse-drawn carriage—a tilbury—Degas and the sculptor Paul-Albert Bartholomé were headed for Diénay, some twenty miles west of Dijon,[1] to stay with their friend Georges Jeanniot, a painter, printer, and the owner of a small château there.[2] At the time, Burgundy was relatively seldom visited by artists in search of scenery; judging from travel literature such as the Baedeker guide, families on holidays or day trips didn't go there either. Burgundy had neither the raw beauty of the Channel coast nor the rustic charm of Brittany, and apparently only one guidebook of the period, the *Guide Joanne* (1874), dared to suggest that there were in fact things to see there: caverns, waterfalls, interesting rock formations.[3] And yet it was here that Degas, an impassioned metropolitan and a sophisticated traveler, created his most important landscape series, a sequence of some fifty color monotypes (prints made in only one copy) executed from copper or zinc plates. Perhaps it was precisely *because* the area lacked time-honored destinations for landscape artists that Degas was able to find in it subjects very personal to him, untouched by other painters.

Degas's Diénay prints are an exceptionally well-documented part of his oeuvre.[4] A detailed hand-drawn map of the route, generally attributed to his companion Bartholomé, survives in the Bibliothèque Nationale de France, and it is illustrated by photographs (taken by their friend Charles de Meixmoron) of the two travelers in the tilbury (fig. 36). In addition, Degas's process in his conception and execution of the monotypes was described in writing by his host Jeanniot.[5] The evening of his arrival in Diénay, it seems, the artist announced his desire to make a group of landscape monotypes, and to use his host's studio for the purpose. He produced the compositions entirely from memory, without the help of any sketches or drawings made during the journey or upon arrival. Yet a print of the Burgundy landscape shows how closely he captured the feeling of its large masses of hills, meadows, and woods (fig. 37).

Created from memory and from the mind rather than in sight of any place they might depict, and intended as a series, these prints are somewhat conceptual in nature, and have the quality of successive shots in a cinematic sequence. They are the traces of images seen en route while moving at a certain pace in the tilbury—fragments of a fleeting vision, quickly noted and impossible to contemplate at length. (It has also been suggested that their almost abstract quality may be related to the eyesight problems from which Degas suffered.[6]) Degas's working process, which grew out of his experience with the medium of etching, made him the prime innovator in the monotype form. It involved the application of oil thinned with turpentine to the copper plate; once the images were printed, he developed some of them further by working in pastel directly on the paper. The dominant presence in these prints is less landscape than color. For the forms of the compositions are mostly devoid of detail; although Degas retained the broad divisions of sky, foliage, fields, or water, he did not render them with any exacting kind of accuracy, and they read as colored shapes on paper no less clearly than they do as trees and hills. Also, the thinned oil was very fluid, and Degas often handled it with his fingertips, creating variations in texture and the effect of spills and pours.

Because the forms that result are strongly generalized, they are open to considerable freedom of interpretation. The viewer's process of perception is as important as the artist's response to the subject. Light and its effects on form play an essential role in the structures of these works, which exquisitely balance light, dark, and the spatial relationships that light and dark suggest. Yet with all this, Degas's Diénay prints do convey an impression of the Burgundy landscape. They cannot be relied upon as a topographical record of it, but they reflect the artist's excitement over what he would come to call his "admirable Burgundy," a place so potent in his imagination that he went back there four times more.

1. On that journey see Richard Kendall, *Degas Landscapes* (New Haven and London: Yale University Press, 1993), pp. 145–81, and Georges Jeanniot, "Souvenirs sur Degas," *Revue Universelle* LV no. 14 (October 15, 1933): 152–74, and no. 15 (November 1, 1933): 281–300.

2. See Kendall, *Degas Landscapes*, p. 145.

3. The *Guide Joanne* was the best-known French guidebook series of the period; after 1912 it became the *Guide Bleu*. See Anne Dumas, "The Public Face of Landscape," in John House, ed., *Landscapes of France: Impressionism and Its Rivals*, exh. cat. (London: Hayward Gallery, 1995), p. 33.

4. See Kendall, *Degas Landscapes*, pp. 146–52, 154–79.

5. See ibid., pp. 145–46.

6. See ibid., p. 152.

Combe, près de Mâlain.

FIGURE 37. *Valley near Mâlain (Combe, près de Mâlain)* from Adolphe Joanne's *Géographie de la Côte d'Or* (Paris, 1874)

PLATE 40 (OPPOSITE). Hilaire-Germain-Edgar Degas. *Green Landscape (Paysage vert).* c. 1890. Monotype, plate: 11 7/8 x 15 11/16" (30.1 x 39.9 cm). The Museum of Modern Art, New York. Louise Reinhardt Smith Bequest

PLATE 41 (OPPOSITE). Hilaire-Germain-Edgar Degas. *A Wooded Landscape (Forêt dans la montagne).* c. 1890. Monotype, plate: 11 7/8 x 15 13/16" (30.1 x 40.2 cm). The Museum of Modern Art, New York. Louise Reinhardt Smith Bequest

FIGURE 36. Artist unknown (Paul-Albert Bartholomé and Charles de Meixmoron?). *Degas's Journey from Paris to Diénay.* 1890. Hand-drawn map and photographs, Bibliothèque Nationale de France, Paris

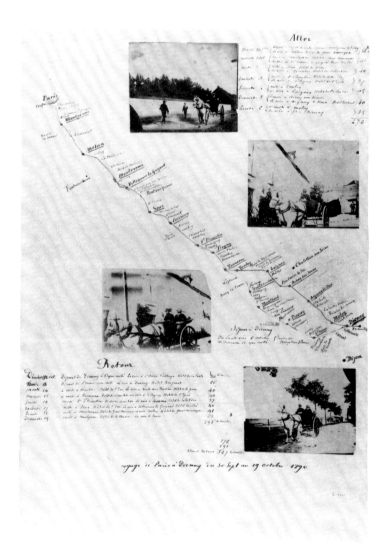

THE SOUTH OF FRANCE

Through much of the nineteenth century, as we have seen, it was sites in the North of France—around Paris, and along the Channel coast—that were the primary subjects of landscape painting. This was partly because so many artists lived in Paris, and also because of the railways, which linked Paris to Normandy in the 1840s. In addition, I would argue, the cool light of the North, whether clear or misty, lent itself to the techniques, the color, and the treatment of surface seen in Impressionist and Neo-Impressionist painting. In the 1880s, however, the railroad system of a more distant region, the South of France, was expanded and developed. As the towns and ports of Provence, the Côte d'Azur, and Languedoc grew more efficiently accessible, they too began to attract artists from other parts of the country.

The South, like Brittany, boasted a strong regional character and a distinctive landscape. It also had a special brilliant light. Its location on the Mediterranean coast brought attractive historical associations with the classical world, and it had begun to emerge as a tourist resort as early as the 1860s. In those years, however, its remoteness made it exclusive: a visit there demanded resources of leisure time unavailable to the working people of the north. The climate, too, was thought hot and uncomfortable in the summer, so that the area had thus far been a tourist destination only in the winter, when the weather was pleasantly mild, and even then only for the affluent.

Paul Cézanne, of course, was a native of Provence, and worked there from the 1860s on. Later, thanks to the railroad, he practically commuted between Provence and Paris. Auguste Renoir visited the South regularly after 1882, then eventually settled there, in 1902; and Claude Monet saw the Côte d'Azur in 1883, and painted at Antibes in 1888. Later, Henri Matisse and almost all of his colleagues in the Fauvist group found the southern landscape and light an inspiration to pictorial innovation. Georges Braque, André Derain, Paul Gauguin, Vincent van Gogh, and Paul Signac were among the many other artists who found motifs in towns like Aix-en-Provence and Arles, in Provence, and Nice, farther east on the Côte d'Azur; in villages like Saint-Rémy-de-Provence and Saint-Tropez; and in the surrounding countryside. For all of these artists, the South's olive groves, cypress trees, rocky ridges, lush gardens, intense blue sky and sea, and wonderful coastline, all bathed in light and heat, were enthralling subjects for landscape art.

AIX-EN-PROVENCE

A native son of Aix-en-Provence, Cézanne analyzed the area's scenery in countless paintings, watercolors, and drawings. Some particular landmarks he returned to again and again: the Jas de Bouffan, his family estate; the village of Gardanne; the Château Noir mansion; the Bibémus quarry; and, surely the most famous of all, the Mont Sainte-Victoire. Studying these same locations from different viewpoints helped Cézanne in his constant effort to reinvent and refine his visual methods and techniques. He sought recognition in Paris and spent a lot of time there over the years, but Provence was always at the center of his activities.

As Cézanne grew older, the art historian John Rewald pointed out, he increasingly confined himself to his most immediate surroundings—that is, to Aix, and particularly to his family's summer residence, the Jas de Bouffan, outside the town.[1] The estate was in the family for some forty years: his father bought it in 1859, when Cézanne was twenty, and it was sold in 1899, after the death of the artist's mother. The house, in Provençal style, dated back to the late seventeenth or early eighteenth century. There were also several outbuildings and a forty-acre park, featuring an orangerie, several fountains, and two impressive allées, one of plane trees, the other of chestnuts, both of them appearing often in Cézanne's paintings.

Reeds at Jas de Bouffan of 1880–82 (plate 42) recalls views in several different parts of the park, for example one shown in a documentary photograph of the allée of chestnut trees (fig. 44). The shrubs and reeds in the left foreground of the watercolor and the trees in the right mid-ground together create a vaulted structure, a tunnellike effect leading the spectator's eye to a long wall in the distance. The combination of horizontals (in the wall), verticals, and diagonals (in the framing reeds and trees) is spatially tense, implying perspective and the illusion of depth. The composition is spare, with expanses of the paper left unpainted, and the empty whites that result inject a feeling of airiness. The simplicity of the color—mainly shades of blue and green—adds to the work's romantic, contemplative mood.[2]

Cézanne spent the autumn and winter of 1885–86 in Gardanne, then a primarily agricultural community set among fields of grain, saffron, and tobacco, and dominated by the bell tower of an eleventh-century church.[3] After his departure, this farming village became an industrial town, for the ground on which it stands contains deposits of both coal and bauxite, and pottery factories and an aluminum forge were built there. In Cézanne's time, though, the red or ocher mineral dust of Gardanne was merely picturesque, giving one part of the village an unusual color. In fact Cézanne admired the beauty of Gardanne, and in a letter he wrote during his stay, to the collector Victor Chocquet, he remarked, "There would be treasures to take away from this countryside here that had not yet found an interpreter on the level of the riches it displays."[4]

The Bridge at Gardanne (plate 43) is one of the works Cézanne produced during the visit of 1885–86. In some ways it describes its site quite objectively (see fig. 45), yet the spacious visual structure, the thinness with which the watercolor has been applied, and the large expanses of paper left unpainted make the subject look weightless. We have a sense of a composition conceived to have a certain pictorial depth, and in fact Cézanne follows a model of foreground, mid-ground, and background familiar since the Renaissance, the different levels being suggested by a tree in the left foreground (a *repoussoir* device) and the curving road leading under the bridge, apparently receding into the distance. Yet the large, flat areas of unpainted paper move the composition toward planarity.

In their near abstraction, later watercolors of Cézanne's such as *Foliage* (plate 44) and *Rocks near the Caves above Le Château Noir* (*Rochers près des grottes au-dessus du Château Noir*; plate 45), both of 1895–1900, presage the history of modern drawing. They are constructions in color—color freed from line, and from the codes of perspective. Cézanne wanted to "realize" nature rather than to depict it through the outlines that are basic to the art of drawing, or through the tonal modeling used in representational drawing or painting to follow a surface's shape.[5] In both of these watercolors, delicately indicated contours provide no more than an armature; the visual structure really inheres in the patches of color applied around them. These layered patches make the space seem to pulsate, a movement emphasized in *Foliage* by the off-balance placement of the forms, all to one side of the image. The object, whether leaves and blossoms or rocks, becomes fugitive; what remains is a perceptual impression or rather a "realization" of the motif, which seems to shimmer in light, for, as in *Reeds at Jas de Bouffan* and *The Bridge at Gardanne*, Cézanne leaves areas of the sheet unpainted, and their white shifts in register, from the materiality of the paper to immaterial brightness. Sketchily specified yet dramatic form is complemented by transparent and fluid color. In *Foliage* in particular the forms have no boundaries; the shapes are open-ended, each one defining and defined by the others around it.

Rocks near the Caves above Le Château Noir is in some ways at the opposite end of the spectrum from *Foliage*—loosely spread out where the other is tightly clustered, tiered and stratified where the other is celled and honeycombed. Yet in each of these works, the attempt to devise a pictorial structure—a rhythmically orchestrated system of surfaces and shapes—is as clear a priority as the attempt to describe an object from or place in the countryside of Cézanne's Provence. *Rocks near the Caves* is one of two very similar watercolors of the same subject, the rock formations at the edge of the Bibémus quarry, some two miles from Aix (fig. 46). The second version, in a private collection in Saint Louis, is vertical rather than horizontal; it seems to have been painted perhaps two hours earlier in the day than *Rocks near the Caves*, and evokes the original site less closely (fig. 38).[6] *Rocks near the Caves* is warm in hue—ochers, brownish reds, violets, touches of green. Delicate brushstrokes trace the swells and hollows in the rock, which undulate rhythmically, the shifts in light on their surfaces evoked by the transparency of the watercolor and the brightness of the white paper where Cézanne has left it bare. There is a feeling of mysterious presence, of a vestige of nature, a universe, becoming abstract, rational, conceptual, yet retaining its physical solidity.

The villa called Château Noir fascinated the older Cézanne. Not a château in the proper sense of the word, this complex of two buildings, set at right angles to each other and surrounded on three sides by a terrace, was built in the second half of the nineteenth century, so that in Cézanne's

1. See John Rewald. "The Last Motifs at Aix," in William Rubin, ed., *Cézanne: The Late Work,* exh. cat. (New York: The Museum of Modern Art, 1977), pp. 83–107.

2. On this work see Rubin and Matthew Armstrong, *The William S. Paley Collection,* exh. cat. (New York: The Museum of Modern Art, 1992), pp. 26–27.

3. On Gardanne see Paul Machotka, *Cézanne: Landscape into Art* (New Haven: Yale University Press, 1996), pp. 66–69, and *Les Sites Cézanniens du pas d'Aix: Hommage à John Rewald* (Paris: Réunion des Musées Nationaux, 1996), pp. 117–27.

4. Paul Cézanne, letter to Victor Chocquet, May 11, 1886, in, *Les Sites Cézanniens du pas d'Aix,* p. 104.

5. Cézanne, quoted in Rewald, "The Last Motifs at Aix," p. 104.

6. See Machotka, *Cézanne: Landscape into Art,* pp. 88–91.

FIGURE 38. Paul Cézanne. ***Rocks near the Caves above Le Château Noir (Rochers près des grottes au-dessus du Château Noir)***. 1895–1900. Pencil and watercolor on paper, 18³/₄ x 11⁷/₈" (47.5 x 30 cm). Collection Mr. and Mrs. Joseph Pulitzer, Saint Louis

time it was fairly new (fig. 47). Set on a steep hill, it was a prominent feature of the region; the slopes of the hill were covered with boulders and lush vegetation, and the warm yellow buildings, made from the stone of the nearby Bibémus quarry, stood out against this dark background. The house was called "*noir*," or "black," not because of its color but because local rumor labeled its builder an alchemist in alliance with the devil. (In fact an alternative name for the house was the "Château du diable.")

After the family estate of Jas de Bouffan was sold, Cézanne tried to acquire Château Noir. He was unsuccessful, but was able to rent a small room in the house, for storage; living in an apartment in Aix, he would come to the house to pick up his materials, and could work outdoors anywhere nearby. Cézanne painted views of Château Noir many times. Setting up his easel in the forest around and above the house, he would invariably show it from a distance, visible over and among the trees. In *Le Château Noir* of 1904–06 (plate 46), the rectilinear architecture, with its yellow walls and red door, stands out against the dark mass of the surrounding woods, rendered by a thick compilation of brushstrokes in shades of green and blue. Yellow and red reverberate again in the mass of rock at the lower left.

The brushstrokes cohere in a dense but vibrant patterning that fills the painting with life. Even when defining the separate planes of the sky and the foliage, they are applied in similar rhythms, often in groups of parallel marks in the same tint. All of the painting's shapes are built up out of these brushstrokes, instead of being outlined by drawn contours. Its firm geometry almost engulfed in the irregular masses of the greenery and sky, the villa seems mysterious, tranquil, and remote. It is interesting to note that the painting originally belonged to Monet, who purchased it directly from Cézanne, and hung it in his bedroom in Giverny.

From the hill of Château Noir, Cézanne had a view of one of the great landmarks of Provence—the Mont Sainte-Victoire, the massive height that overlooks the valley of the River Arc. In a letter of 1878 to his friend Emile Zola, Cézanne wrote,

"An astounding motif arises on the East: Ste-Victoire and the rocks that dominate Beaurecueil. I said: what a beautiful motif."[7] Between 1885 and 1906, the year of his death, Cézanne painted over forty views of Mont Sainte-Victoire, from different locations and in different mediums: oil, watercolor, pencil. The works vary in the details, but that majestic shape rising into the sky is always instantly recognizable. A favorite place for Cézanne's studies of the mountain was a spot on the east side of the Château Noir terrace. Rewald took numerous documentary photographs around here in 1935, and wrote, "When he followed the terrace to the east, he reached a shady grove where the view toward Sainte-Victoire was unhampered, with not a house in sight, nothing but vineyards, fields dotted with dark cypresses, woods, and hills behind which rises the mountain, its massive, chopped-off cone barring the horizon."[8]

In 1901–02, Cézanne built a studio for himself on the hill of Les Lauves, which overlooks Aix, to the south, and a breathtaking sweep of Provence countryside culminating in the mass of Mont Sainte-Victoire, to the east. A loosely painted watercolor from 1902–06 (plate 47) shows this latter view, seen not from the studio but from the hilltop above it—the site of a number of Cézanne's late landscapes, in which Mont Sainte-Victoire returns repeatedly, an iconic image.

The mountain fills the top third of the sheet, establishing a high horizon line against a delicately painted sky. The bushes and rocks in the foreground are rendered in transparent shades of blues, greens, pale pinks, and lavenders, all highlighted by open expanses of unpainted paper. Sainte-Victoire itself is partly lavender, but its frontal scarp is almost all bare paper, suggesting a bleached white, and a time of day when the sun is high and bright, and the shadows so dark they look purple. Cézanne's brushstrokes energize the work's surface; handling the watercolor pigment with great freedom, which conveys an intensity of feeling, he structures the composition not through line but through color, arriving at a complete "realization" of the motif. The scene is imposing and dramatic, the mountain seeming to float in the southern sun above the fields and farms. This was the landscape that inspired Cézanne in his invention of a modern pictorial language.

ARLES

Not all of the artists who came to Provence fell in love with it. In late 1888, Paul Gauguin spent two months in Arles, some forty miles west of Aix. He was visiting Vincent van Gogh, who had come for a longer stay. Van Gogh was fascinated by the light and color of the region—in fact he dreamed of creating an artists' colony there. Gauguin, on the other hand, disliked the place from the start.[9] (Perhaps he had been hoping for the lush tropical scenery he must have remembered from his childhood in Peru, and from his later travels to Martinique, India, and other ports of call as a member of the merchant marine.) Nevertheless, despite his dislike for Provence, and the difficulty of coping with van Gogh's volatile personality, Gauguin produced a number of works in various mediums during his relatively brief time in the region.

7. Cézanne, letter to Emile Zola, April 14, 1878, in Rewald, ed., *Paul Cézanne: Letters* (London: Bruno Cassirer, 1941), p. 114.

8. Rewald, "The Last Motifs at Aix," p. 90.

9. See the letter from Paul Gauguin to Emile Bernard, quoted in *Peintres de la couleur en Provence 1875–1920*, exh. cat. (Paris: Réunion des Musées Nationaux, 1995), p. 242.

FIGURE 39. Le Pouldu, n.d. Postcard

Arles is actually a striking place, an old Roman town on the Rhône, with a spectacular arena and theater from the classical period. Another important landmark is the cathedral of Saint Trophîme, built between the eleventh and the fifteenth centuries. Thirty-odd years before van Gogh came to Arles, Edouard-Denis Baldus applied a camera to the challenge of describing the town's strange beauty (plate 49). Photography can be a literal medium, crammed with the factual detail of the visible world; in Arles, however, Baldus was moved to evoke hidden presences, for he made his subject a relic from the town's ancient days, a Roman graveyard, compact symbol of both a history lost to time and a community lost to mortality.

In addition to the Rhône, Arles has three canals, and here, in the spring and summer of 1888, van Gogh painted what must then have been a common scene in the town but now has a quality of "local color": washerwomen at work on the water's bank. When Gauguin arrived in October, he painted the same motif, twice, and one of these works is now in the collection of The Museum of Modern Art (plate 48). Four women kneel in a line by the edge of the Roubine du Roi canal, while others, their work over, leave to the left. They wear the traditional costume of the women of Arles, which appears quite similar to the clothes of the Breton women Gauguin had seen earlier that year in Pont-Aven and Le Pouldu (fig. 39). The kneeling woman who wears no bonnet or head-wrap may be Madame Ginoux, the *arlésienne* who appears in related works by Gauguin and van Gogh, and who owned the Café de la Gare, where van Gogh rented a room on his arrival in the town.

With its row of evenly spaced figures in orderly recession, their placement matched by the line of trees on the water's opposite bank, the painting is almost classical in its arrangement. Indeed the underlying structure of the composition is strongly geometric. Suspended in their activity, the figures of the women have a hieratic quality—not only in their formal order, but in their kneeling stance's suggestion of some kind of religious observance. This bent-over obeisance contrasts with the pose of the upright figure at the left, which also stabilizes the composition by extending the regular row of verticals constituted by the trees on the far bank.

Gauguin uses the Synthetist style he had developed at Pont-Aven, characterized by areas of flat, relatively unmodulated color contained within simple and definite contours. The result is a decorative, patternlike quality, as if the different elements of the picture had been fitted together like a jigsaw. This also has the effect of making the figures seem to blend into the landscape. Just as the peasants Gauguin had painted in Brittany represented for him a primeval communion between humankind and nature, the women of Arles become symbols of France's rural tradition, of a hardworking but proud peasant folk in harmony with their environment.

Saint-Rémy-de-Provence

Van Gogh, unlike Gauguin, delighted in Provence. It was his great misfortune, however, to become seriously ill there, suffering a nervous attack generally believed to have been a symptom of epilepsy. Gauguin's visit, also, ended in tension and quarrel. In May of 1889, then, van Gogh voluntarily committed himself to the asylum of Saint-Paul-de-Mausole, about two miles outside Saint-Rémy-de-Provence and some twenty miles to the northeast of Arles. He would remain there for a little over a year.

Right from the start of his time at Saint-Paul-de-Mausole, van Gogh was allowed to paint, taking one of the building's empty rooms as a studio and also working in the garden. Nor was he confined to the asylum: within about a month, accompanied by a guard, he was leaving its walls to paint in the fields beyond. As he wrote to his brother Theo in Paris, about two weeks after his arrival, "The country round Saint-Rémy is very beautiful and little by little I shall probably widen my field of endeavor."[10]

In Arles, van Gogh had seen a lush landscape of orchards, wheat fields, and vineyards. Saint-Rémy lies in less prosperous countryside, where wheat and grapes give way to a region of bare rugged hills scattered with olive groves and cypresses, all laid out under the rough skyline of the Alpilles mountains. The stands of olive and cypress trees would become crucial motifs in van Gogh's paintings of Saint-Rémy, and appear respectively in two important works in the collection of The Museum of Modern Art. Around June 18, 1889, van Gogh scrupulously reported to Theo that he had at last completed "a landscape with olive trees and also a new study of a starry night"[11]; the first of these was *The Olive Trees* (plate 50), the second *The Starry Night* (plate 51). Although van Gogh's letter falls short of describing the two paintings as pendants, it does suggest he saw them as a pair.

The Olive Trees sets the gnarled, even tortured shapes of the olive boughs against the backdrop of the steep Alpilles. This range of mountains is dominated by two striking peaks, both of which the painting shows, Les Deux Trous on the left and Mont Gaussier on the right (fig. 49). Of the several paintings of Provençal olive trees that van Gogh produced, this is the only one unmistakably describing a specific place in the Saint-Rémy landscape; the others are more generalized.[12] Yet the work is completely a personal vision, for there is nothing strictly realistic about the swirling rhythms of the soil, the tree trunks, the hills, and the coiling white cloud, all determined in their expressive tenor by the palette of cool blue green. Writing again on these two works in September of 1889, van Gogh himself told Theo, "The olive trees with the white cloud and the mountains behind, as well as the rise of the moon and the night effect, are exaggerations....the outlines are accentuated."[13] In his earlier letter he had suggested that the two works derived "more from Delacroix than might appear,"[14] but he also recognized that in their stylized lines and less-than-naturalistic use of color they more immediately reflected the principles of Emile Bernard and Gauguin, both members of the Pont-Aven school. Bernard and Gauguin, van Gogh wrote, "do not care at all about the exact form of a tree, but they do insist that one should

10. Vincent van Gogh, letter to his brother Theo, May 22, 1889, quoted in Ronald Pickvance, *Van Gogh in Saint Rémy and Auvers,* exh. cat. (New York: The Metropolitan Museum of Art, 1986), p. 30.

11. Van Gogh, letter to Theo, June 18, 1889, quoted in ibid., p. 33.

12. See Pickvance, *Van Gogh in Saint Rémy and Auvers,* p. 101–2.

13. Van Gogh, letter to Theo, mid-September 1889, quoted in Rewald, *Post-Impressionism: From van Gogh to Gauguin* (New York: The Museum of Modern Art, 1978), p. 322.

14. Van Gogh, letter to Theo, quoted in ibid., p. 312. Rewald dates this letter to June 19, 1889, Pickvance to June 18, 1889.

FIGURE 40. Vincent van Gogh. *Mountainous Landscape behind the Asylum*. 1889. Oil on canvas, 28 x 35" (70.5 x 88.5 cm). Ny Carlsberg Glyptotek, Copenhagen

be able to say whether its form is round or square....They won't ask for the exact color of mountains, but they will say, 'Damn it, those mountains, were they blue? Well then, make them blue and don't tell me that it was a blue a little bit like this or a little bit like that....make them blue and that's all!'"[15]

An aerial view of St-Paul-de-Mausole, from a postcard of the 1940s (fig. 50), shows nearby fields planted with olive trees, most clearly on the picture's right. In the mid-ground we may also identify the slender tops of cypress trees, a prominent motif in *The Starry Night*. Van Gogh seems to have wanted to paint the stars virtually on his arrival at the asylum—the window of his room looked out on a vast sweep of night sky. He had already painted such a picture in Arles the previous September. Now he was inspired to do so again.

The Starry Night, however, unlike *The Olive Trees*, does not seem to have been painted in direct observation of its subject, for it is a composite of several motifs, not all of them visible in any single view from the asylum. In fact van Gogh seems to have conflated elements from two slightly earlier works, *Mountainous Landscape behind the Asylum* (fig. 40) and *Wheat Field* (fig. 41). Variations on the form of the cypress tree on the left feature in a number of his pictures from Saint-Rémy, and in fact had already appeared occasionally, in less prominent roles, in canvases he had done in Arles. Although the sky in *The Starry Night*, including the positions of the stars and the silhouette of the mountains, resembles the view from the window of van Gogh's room, the cypress is his

FIGURE 41. Vincent van Gogh. *Wheat Field.* 1889. Oil on canvas, 29 x 36 ¹/₂" (73.5 x 92.5 cm). Národní Galerie, Prague

addition. (The room he used as a studio, also, where he presumably painted this work, looks out in a different direction.) The village, too, although it bears a relation to the view of Saint-Rémy seen in the postcard, looks less like Provence than like Holland, where van Gogh was born and grew up. This is particularly clear in the church spire at the picture's center—entirely an invented addition, and one that plants in the southern landscape an element of the north. (Van Gogh had painted similar churches when he still lived in Holland.) The vertical, elongated form of the spire parallels the soaring cypress tree in the left foreground, lifting the eye to the swirling night sky.

Van Gogh discussed his fascination with the cypress tree in one of his letters to Theo: "They are beautiful in line and proportion like an Egyptian obelisk. And the green has such a distinguished quality. It is the black spot in a sunlit landscape."[16] In Mediterranean countries, cypress trees are traditionally planted in cemeteries, and are associated with death and the afterlife. (They signify as opposites, then, of another of van Gogh's favorite motifs, the sunflower.) To pair them with a night sky seems to magnify this symbolism—which is not to say that *The Starry Night* is dark or morbid. In fact the painting vibrates with life. Observation fuses with invention, heightened color with animate visual rhythm. Dynamic and luminous, the sky rises in powerful counterpoint to the dark green, almost black of the cypresses. *The Olive Trees* has been discussed as a religious picture, a somber

15. Van Gogh, letter to Theo, mid-September 1889, quoted in ibid., p. 322.

16. Van Gogh, letter to Theo, quoted in Pickvance, *Van Gogh in Saint Rémy and Auvers,* p. 108.

image of spiritual longing and struggle, with somewhere implicit in it the memory of the Mount of Olives and the garden of Gethsemane.[17] *The Starry Night* is no less suggestive: the upward-straining cypress seems to link earth to heaven, and the rural landscape to embody the eternal life of the natural world.

THE CÔTE D'AZUR: NICE, SAINT-RAPHAEL, SAINT-TROPEZ

The stretch of the Mediterranean coast extending from the Italian border at Menton to Cannes—the so-called French Riviera— became a tourist resort during the Second Empire, in the 1860s, but its coast and climate had captivated artists well before then. Nice, a center of artistic and intellectual life for the South of France, had attracted landscape painters as early as the end of the eighteenth century;[18] Eugène Delacroix stayed there in the 1830s, Monet in 1883. Nice is a town of superb local color and particularly of light—the special light of the Midi, which crystallizes form, gives brilliance and fullness to color, and eliminates shadows. Here, at the end of 1917, Henri Matisse came to live.

Matisse stayed in Nice and its environs until the end of his life, in 1954, but what is referred to as his "Nice period" is primarily the decade of the 1920s, when he was painting hot-colored, thickly decorated interiors inhabited by languorous odalisques and suffused with light. The style of these works, which actually emerged virtually on his arrival in Nice, was more naturalistic and apparently more conservative than his work had been during the years 1905–17, the period first of his innovative Fauvist canvases and later of his development in parallel with Cubism. Perhaps as an effect of an intense correspondence with Monet, and of the proximity of Pierre-Auguste Renoir, who was living at Cagnes, Matisse had renewed his interest in Impressionism, the innovative landscape art of this older generation. Although ornamented interiors predominate in his work of the decade or so after World War I, views of land and sea also appear, and constitute an important group of paintings.

Landscape of 1918 (plate 52) belongs to a group of works painted in the Paillon valley, where Matisse is said to have worked *en plein air, sur le motif,* as the French would say, on the slopes of Mont Boron and Mont Alban, looking toward the small villas on the Mediterranean coast. He would often finish the works later in the studio. Only a year before, working out of his home in the Paris suburb of Issy-les-Moulineaux in the spring and summer of 1917, he had been producing such works as *Shaft of Sunlight, the Woods of Trivaux* (fig. 42), an austere, angular, almost abstract composition informed by elements of Cubism and by northern light. *Landscape,* by contrast, is intimate in atmosphere and scale, conveying the silvery light that Matisse associated with Nice. The artist is looking into a thicket of curving trees silhouetted against grayish sky, and apparently lit from within by a soft yellow glow. Patches of lighter green indicate sunlit grass; there is the feeling of a quiet, sheltered enclave of nature. "Ah!," Matisse once wrote, "Nice is a beautiful place. What a gentle and soft light in spite of its brightness!...Touraine light is a little more golden. Here it is silvered. Even the objects that it touches are very colored, such as the greens for example."[19]

17. Van Gogh himself had these references in mind during this period, although he did not want to make them explicit; see Rewald, *Post-Impressionism,* p. 338.

18. See *Peintres de la couleur en Provence, 1875–1920.*

19. Henri Matisse, letter to Charles Camoin, May 23, 1918, quoted in Jack Cowart, "The Place of Silvered Light: An Expanded Illustrated Chronology of Matisse in the South of France, 1916–1932," in Cowart and Dominique Fourcade, *Henri Matisse: The Early Years in Nice, 1916–1930,* exh. cat. (Washington, D.C.: National Gallery of Art, and New York: Harry N. Abrams, 1986), p. 22.

Another artist who came from the north to the Midi, in search of light and color, was Louis Valtat. He was a native of Dieppe, near the Normandy port towns frequented, we have seen, by Impressionist painters such as Monet and by Neo-Impressionists such as Seurat, but he was a member of the younger generation that discovered the South. (He was born in 1869, the same year as Matisse.) Valtat first visited the Mediterranean coast in 1897, and went back there in the two years following. In 1902, 1903, and 1904, he stayed in Saint-Tropez, with Signac, and his *Landscape* of 1904 (plate 53) depicts a spot on the coast nearby, at Saint-Raphael.

A recent photograph of Saint-Raphael (fig. 52) suggests how close the swirling pictorial rhythms of Valtat's picture come to the mood of this rocky and craggy place. The greens, pinks, blues, and yellows of his palette are also strikingly exact in reflecting the local color of the area, known as the Côte d'Esterel. The painting's sinuous lines, and its massing of volumes in the depiction of rocks and greenery, reflect the influence of both the Nabis (the Symbolist group that included Ker-Xavier Roussel, discussed elsewhere in this book) and Art Nouveau. There are also traces of pointillist technique, which Valtat probably introduced under the sway of his friend Signac. The large brushstrokes of heavily applied color unify the surface, and make even the small whitish-yellow figure part of the landscape.

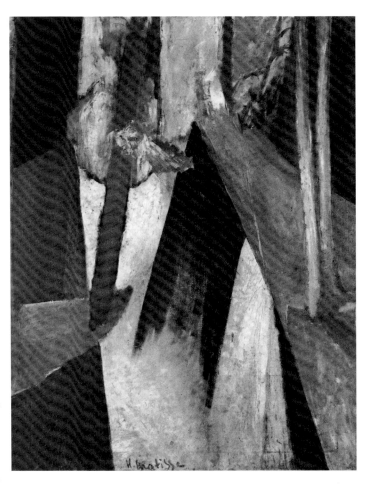

FIGURE 42. Henri Matisse. *Shaft of Sunlight, the Woods of Trivaux.* 1917. Oil on canvas, 36 x 29¹/₈" (91 x 74 cm). Private collection

The problems of conveying the relationship between color and light in the South of France, and of using color and light to render space, come intensely to the fore in a number of paintings, watercolors, and prints executed in Saint-Tropez. Signac "discovered" the town, then a small fishing port, in 1892, during a sailing trip along the coast. In October of 1893 he bought a house there, and for the next decade, dividing his time between Saint-Tropez and Paris, he invited many friends to enjoy the beauty of the place. This was where Valtat was staying when he painted *Landscape*; Matisse spent a summer nearby in 1904.

Two lithographs by Signac, *The Buoy (Saint-Tropez Harbor)* (*La Bouée [Saint-Tropez: Le Port]*) of 1894 (plate 55) and *Port of Saint-Tropez* (*Port de Saint-Tropez*) of 1898 (plate 54), present views of the port that are clearly recognizable in a postcard from the period (fig. 53).

In color they are opposites, *The Buoy* very bright, its shifting carpet of blues broken by blocks of yellow and yellow-orange that seem to coalesce and catch fire in the deep red of the buoy in the foreground, while *Port of Saint-Tropez* is all pale hues of blue and lemon yellow. But both works show Signac's concern with the power of color. The palette of *The Buoy* vividly suggests the heat and brightness of strong midday sun; in *Port of Saint-Tropez* Signac softens that heat into a pastel glow over the bell tower and surrounding buildings, suggesting a place no less sun-flooded but less fierce, more sensuous, all coolly reflected in the dancing waters of the harbor. With their surfaces broken into an interlocking network of discrete dabs and marks, the works also demonstrate Signac's admiration for the work of Monet and more particularly Seurat, as well as his interest in the color theories of both artists (Delacroix) and scientists (Eugène Chevreul and Ogden Rood), theories emphasizing the interplay of colors and their complementaries to achieve expressive effect.

Saint-Tropez also appealed to Matisse, who went there with his wife, Amélie, and son Pierre in July of 1904 to spend the summer near Signac, whom he had met earlier that year. He remained in Saint-Tropez until late September, painting several works in a style influenced by Cézanne. One of these works, *The Gulf of Saint-Tropez*, would provide the foundation for *Luxe, calme et volupté* (fig. 8), which Matisse painted back in Paris during the autumn and winter of 1904–05. He also painted a preparatory study for *Luxe, calme et volupté*, and it is this study that is in the collection of The Museum of Modern Art (plate 56).

Luxe, calme et volupté was the first composition of figures that Matisse created from his imagination, as opposed to from the model. Amélie and Pierre appear in *The Gulf of Saint-Tropez*, and the figure of Amélie remains in the later pair of works; Pierre, however, is replaced by (or transformed into) a woman, and the other bathers Matisse invented. The subject is a beachside picnic, identified as such by the cloth and tableware spread out at the lower left. But *Luxe, calme et volupté* is not a genre painting—it transports the viewer into an arcadian environment, "a sort of paradise," John Elderfield has written, "an atemporal island arcadia reachable only by boat, like Cythera" in the famous painting by Watteau (fig. 4).[20] This dreamlike aspect is confirmed by the title of the work, a quotation from Baudelaire's poem "*L'Invitation au voyage*," in which the poet invites his mistress to abandon the ordinary world and follow him to an ideal land made up in her image: "There," writes Baudelaire, "all is only order and beauty, / Luxury, calm, and sensual delight" (*Là, tout n'est qu'ordre et beauté, / Luxe, calme et volupté*). Matisse named the painting only after its completion, as an afterthought,[21] but even without the title the sense would remain of an ideal world that can only be gained through a process of imagination and reverie. There is a layering of imagery and meaning: a specific physical location is transformed into a vision, a dream of an unknowable paradise.

In 1898–99, Matisse had briefly experimented with Neo-Impressionism, constructing his images out of small dots or dabs of paint. Now, as a result of conversations with Signac, he decided to attempt the approach again: both *Luxe, calme et volupté* and the study for it are executed in a version of the Neo-Impressionist style, using rather larger, more rectangular brushstrokes than those of its original practitioners, notably Seurat. A methodical system of pictorial marks is applied in a bricklike accretion to create a uniform surface. In its formal structure, its relationships of horizontals, verticals, and diagonals, the picture is organized according to the rules of the Golden Section, which enhances the remoteness and timelessness of the scene even as the landscape behind the figural grouping is specific and recognizable.[22] The colors too, laid pure on the canvas to mix in the viewer's eye (instead of premixed to the appropriate shade on the palette), produce an aura of unreality.

Luxe, calme et volupté revives and rephrases such earlier traditions as the pastorals of sixteenth-century Italy and the *fêtes champêtres* and *fêtes galantes* of eighteenth-century France, as well as more recent arcadian landscapes such as those of Puvis de Chavannes.[23] It is a modern, secularized adaptation of the theme of the golden age. Executed in a modernist idiom, landscape becomes the vehicle of a new vision, its mixture of the real and the dreamlike opening it to many levels of interpretation. In color the painting both advances the experiment of the divisionist technique, developed by Seurat some twenty years earlier, and leads directly to something new—Fauvism, the art movement born the following summer in another small town in the South, the Catalan port of Collioure.

L'ESTAQUE

A particularly inspiring place for modernist landscape artists was the Mediterranean village of L'Estaque, near Marseilles. Cézanne worked here on and off from 1870 to the mid-1880s, Braque and Derain during their Fauvist period in 1906–07, and Braque again in 1908, when his style was moving into what would later be known as Cubism. The railroad from Avignon to Marseilles passes through L'Estaque; built in the 1840s, it gave the village a train station, a viaduct, and the Nerthe tunnel (the longest in France). Its completion also permitted train travel all the way between Marseilles and Paris. Inevitably, the railroad changed L'Estaque, bringing elements of modernity into a rural scene. Yet this beautiful village and bay, and the light that made the colors of the landscape so unexpectedly luminous and intense, attracted artists for decades.

Cézanne first summered in L'Estaque in 1864. He may have visited again in 1869, and certainly stayed for a longer period from July of 1870 to March of 1871, during the Franco-Prussian War. Later visits came in 1876, 1878, 1879, 1882, and 1883. When working in the village, Cézanne often chose a high vantage point; in *L'Estaque* (1882–83; plate 58) he positioned himself on a hill above the house where he was staying. In May of 1882, he had written to his friend Emile Zola in Paris, "I have rented a small house with a garden in L'Estaque, just above the railroad station, at the bottom of a hill, where the cliffs with pines begin behind me....I have here beautiful viewpoints."[24] He would paint the view of the Bay of Marseilles from the house and the hill above it many times.

L'Estaque is densely structured, and compared to other works Cézanne produced here, its color is rather sober. The high horizon line of the sea,

20. John Elderfield, *Henri Matisse: A Retrospective*, exh. cat. (New York: The Museum of Modern Art, 1992), p. 33.

21. Ibid. See also Jack Flam, *Matisse: The Man and His Art, 1869–1918* (Ithaca and London: Cornell University Press, 1986), pp. 114–21.

22. Elderfield, *Matisse in the Collection of The Museum of Modern Art*, exh. cat. (New York: The Museum of Modern Art, 1978), p. 36. Another artist's concern with the Golden Section is discussed in Alan Lee, "Seurat and Science," *Art History* 10 no. 2 (June 1987).

23. More recent arcadian visions include Paul Signac's painting *Au Temps de Harmonie*, reproduced in *Signac et la libération de la couleur: de Matisse à Mondrian*, exh. cat. (Paris: Réunion des Musées Nationaux, 1997), p. 58, and Puvis de Chavannes's painting *The Pleasant Land*, in Robert L. Herbert, *Impressionism: Art, Leisure and Parisian Society* (New Haven and London: Yale University Press, 1988), p. 253.

24. Cézanne, letter to Zola, May 24, 1883, in Rewald, ed., *Paul Cézanne: Letters*.

the vertical trees on the left with the smaller, more distant church spire visually adjoining them, and the steeply slanting forms of the cliffs at the right create a scaffolding or frame within which Cézanne groups the remaining elements of the landscape. This clear structure leads the viewer's eye through the otherwise compressed composition toward the open space in the background. The composition also depends on strong diagonals, made by the rooflines of houses running up from the center of the painting toward the left, and by the lines of coast and hill that rise to the right. This structure, it has been pointed out, of a V-shape meeting near the bottom of the composition and relatively close to the picture plane, inverts the familiar perspectival principle in which diagonals meet at a vanishing point deep in the pictorial field.[25] Cézanne's "constructive stroke"—his groups of short parallel brushstrokes in close colors—adds to the tightness of the composition. It is interesting to note that L'Estaque, designed according to principles that are quite cerebral in relation to the more spontaneous conceptions of Impressionism, was acquired in 1896 by Monet, and remained in his house at Giverny until well after his death.

The twenty-odd years after 1885 saw vigorous expansion in L'Estaque. With the growth of a chemical industry accompanying the exploitation of local minerals, factory buildings and an industrial loading dock came to the village. There was also a growth in tourism, which led to the construction of several elegant hotels drawing an international clientele. But the scenery continued to attract artists, and when Derain came to L'Estaque in the summer of 1906, he could still say, in a letter to Matisse, "Here the sites are very pretty. The light is brighter than at Collioure, but equally soft. The landscape is not equally picturesque nor so Italian as that of Collioure, yet in the distance there are chalky mountains, covered with pines, which are superb in their wildness and luminosity."[26]

Collioure was the town, farther west on the Mediterranean coast, where Derain had spent the summer of 1905. Working there alongside Matisse, he had been deeply involved in the development of Fauvism, an advanced style of painting predicated on the use of intense color. (The name "Fauves"—or "Wild beasts"—derives from the spontaneous response of the critic Louis Vauxcelles to the work of the Fauvist painters; at the time, many considered their palette outrageously lurid.) At the beginning of Derain's stay at L'Estaque, however, he seems to have gone through a creative crisis, and his work underwent a distinct evolution there: although suffused with bright color, the fifteen or so canvases he painted that August and early September show the influence of Cézanne (whose earlier presence in L'Estaque must have been in Derain's thoughts) through their dependence on an underlying structure, rather than a structure supplied mainly through color.

L'Estaque (plate 59) remains quite close in style to the pictures Derain had painted at Collioure the previous summer, particularly in its surface, a mosaiclike construction of small dabs and strokes. It must have been painted early in Derain's stay in the village, but he was already moving toward larger brushstrokes, broader areas of color, and more-uniform pictorial marks. The high horizon line recalls Cézanne's L'Estaque of 1882–83, discussed above, but the areas of color seem inspired by the work of

Gauguin, which Derain had seen in a large retrospective at the Salon d'automne of 1903, and perhaps also in 1905 at the house of Daniel de Monfreid, a friend of Gauguin's whom Derain and Matisse had visited while they were staying in Collioure. Although the painting recognizably depicts a place on the shore in L'Estaque (see fig. 54), the specificity of the site is of secondary importance to the brightness and luminosity of the landscape.

Bridge over the Riou (plate 60) shows further development in Derain's style. The shapes are larger, and are more often defined by outlines around their edges (a device revealing the influence of Gauguin still more strongly than the colors of *L'Estaque*); the palette allows for a wider range of tones. (The year before, like the other Fauves, Derain had favored purer colors.) Firm verticals and the diagonals that slant upward from the left and right edges toward the center of the painting create a clear pictorial structure, but the space is shallow enough that the foreground and background forms seem to press against each other. Color bears little relation to the colors of nature—Derain may use an indian red or pink, say, for a tree trunk—so that it takes on a decorative aspect. The softly curving trees draw arabesques across the canvas.

Bridge over the Riou is the second of three works that Derain based on the same scene. (The other two are *Three Trees, L'Estaque* [*Trois arbres, L'Estaque*], in a private collection, and *The Turning Road, L'Estaque* [*L'Estaque. Route tournante*], in The Museum of Fine Arts, Houston.) All of them recognizably resemble the topography of the site, but they were executed in the studio rather than painted *en plein air*, and Derain himself pointed out their artifice by calling them "compositions."[27] With its brilliant palette, rich forms, inventive organization, and intensity of mood, *Bridge over the Riou* is among the most advanced of Derain's paintings from these years. His pictorial language stands among the most innovative in modernist landscape art.

After Derain's summer in L'Estaque in 1906, Braque stayed in the village from October of that year through February of 1907. Another northerner who was to be lastingly affected by the Mediterranean landscape, Braque was born in Argenteuil, outside Paris, and grew up in Le Havre, on the Normandy coast, where he developed a love for the northern light along the shore of the English Channel. His visit to L'Estaque, however, introduced him to the richness of southern light. Fascinated by the Midi generally, he was particularly attracted to L'Estaque because of its association with Cézanne,[28] whose work was a crucial influence on him.

With its exuberant color and curvilinear forms, *The Great Trees, L'Estaque* (1906–07; plate 61) represents Braque's version of Fauvism. More than the other Fauvist painters generally did, he structures the picture sturdily, unifying it with the series of undulating lines and forms that run through it. The large central trees have an almost iconic presence, yet there is also a decorative aspect to the color and the interlocking forms. A documentary photograph of L'Estaque (fig. 56) suggests the kind of landscape that inspired Braque here, but our appreciation of the painting does not depend on such knowledge of the site; the stylistic and spatial liberties Braque takes—the unreal colors, the

25. See Rubin, *The William S. Paley Collection*, p. 28.

26. André Derain, letter to Matisse, August 2, 1906, in *Henri Matisse, 1904–1917*, exh. cat. (Paris: Centre Georges Pompidou/Musée d'art moderne, 1993), p. 76.

27. Derain, *Lettres à Vlaminck*, ed. Maurice de Vlaminck (Paris: Flammarion, 1955), pp. 146–47.

28. See Georges Braque's remarks in Jacques Lassaigne, "Entretiens avec Braque," excerpt from an interview with Braque in 1961, in *Les Cubistes*, exh. cat. (Bordeaux: Musée des Beaux-Arts, 1973).

FIGURE 43. Georges Braque. *Houses at L'Estaque.* 1908. Oil on canvas, 28³/₄ x 23¹/₂" (73 x 60 cm). Romilly 14. Kunstmuseum Bern. Hermann and Margrit Rupf Foundation

distorted perspectives—give the picture a nonspecific quality. The composition's tight weave of horizontals, verticals, and diagonals reflect the artist's understanding of the compositional principles of Cézanne. Color is used here not only for its emotional or decorative qualities but for its ability to build a pictorial structure.

Braque made a number of visits to L'Estaque in these years, one of them in the summer of 1908, when he stayed from mid-May to late September. The influence of Cézanne is still more pronounced in his work of this period. As William Rubin has pointed out, the several paintings he produced here to exhibit at the Salon d'automne, later in the year, fall into two groups, one elaborating the style of 1906–07, the other an early but fully developed mode of Cubism.[29] *Road near L'Estaque* (plate 62) falls into this second group, which would culminate in *Houses at L'Estaque* (fig. 43).

Probably painted during the latter part of Braque's stay in the South that summer, *Road near L'Estaque* reveals an entirely new pictorial language. The road turns and climbs, a parapet running along its edge. The nearer of its turns is shown by the way it seems to tip down until it is almost parallel with the picture plane. The shadows are angled and geometric, and indeed much of the picture seems to be made up of faceted straight-edged planes; the schematized trees, and the folds of the hillside, create an almost abstract surface pattern. The space is shallow, and the palette, so bright the year before, is kept to blues, grays, greens, and ochers—the colors of early Cubism. Braque was interested, he said, in the "materialization of the space," the tangibility of space and form.[30] He builds the picture out of the contrast of light and shadow. A brushwork of parallel strokes, inspired by Cézanne, unifies the surface and gives it tightness and tension.

Seen alongside *The Great Trees, L'Estaque* of the year before, *Road near L'Estaque* demonstrates clearly how remarkable a leap Braque had made in the development of a modernist language—and he made this leap while exploring a landscape motif. Conceived not on-site but in the studio, perhaps using earlier studies and recollections of a specific place, the work emphasizes the cerebral and conceptual side of the creative process. Braque's work in L'Estaque that summer of 1908 marked a major breakthrough in the history of modern art.

LA CIOTAT

Between the two visits to the South that produced *The Great Trees*, *L'Estaque* and *Road near L'Estaque*, Braque spent the summer of 1907 in La Ciotat, a resort town near Marseilles, beautifully recorded in a photograph by Baldus some fifty years earlier (plate 63). In L'Estaque in 1906–07, Braque had lightened his palette and, under the influence of Cézanne, had tightened his composition. These qualities are apparent in the works he painted in La Ciotat. While color is increasingly important, it is not the principal agent of expression; line, structure, and the internal organization of the painting bear their own considerable weight.

Landscape at La Ciotat (plate 64), which Braque painted that summer of 1907, has the expressiveness of color associated with the Fauves. Its predominant yellow suggests a countryside suffused with sun and light, but the composition is rigorous in structure. The landscape is defined by strong contours, and instead of appearing to recede as they mount toward the high horizon line, its elements mass and bulk as they climb the canvas, as if, rather than growing more distant, they were simply arranged on different levels. Braque's interest here is structural as much as chromatic—he puts color not to decorative but to constructive use, moderating its exuberance through the undulating curvilinear elements with which he holds the picture together. The use of large areas of flat unmodulated color brings Gauguin to mind, as well as Matisse's great Fauve composition *Le Bonheur de vivre* of 1905–06 (fig. 9).

SÈTE

Sète lies to the west of the Côte d'Azur, in Languedoc, not far from Montpellier and Béziers. It is not a pretty fishing village but a trading port (after Marseilles, the most important French port on the Mediterranean), nor is it an old town by the standards of the region, and in the late nineteenth century it was not much frequented by either artists or tourists. Yet the Belgian artist Theo van Rysselberghe came here in 1892, and painted *The Port of Sète* (*Le Port de Cette*; plate 65).

The Port of Sète is executed in a Neo-Impressionist idiom that van Rysselberghe developed after visiting Paris, in 1886, to see the first exhibition of Seurat's *Sunday Afternoon on the Island of La Grande Jatte* (fig. 12). The audacious novelty of that great work, and Seurat's rational treatment of color and disciplined approach to composition, drew the young artist to experiment with Neo-Impressionism himself. His friendship with Signac, a follower of Seurat's, strengthened his involvement in the techniques of pointillism and divisionism, and he too learned to apply complementary colors in carefully weighed combinations so as to enhance each other and mix in the viewer's eye.

When Signac sailed the Côte d'Azur in 1892, and stopped for the first time in the port of Saint-Tropez, van Rysselberghe was with him on his boat, the *Olympia*. The Belgian artist visited Sète during that same trip. As a northerner, he was excited by the light of the South and its reflections on the water, and *The Port of Sète* has an overall blue tonality, with flickers of white and yellow, that conveys this Mediterranean ambience. Crowds of boats and thickets of masts reflect the atmosphere of a commercial

29. See Rubin, "Cézannisme and the Beginnings of Cubism," in Rubin, ed., *Cézanne: The Late Work*. Also see the slightly revised version of this essay published in *L'Estaque: Naissance du paysage moderne, 1870–1910*, exh. cat. (Marseilles: Musées de Marseille, Réunion des Musées Nationaux, 1994), p. 47.

30. Braque, quoted in Rubin, "Cézannisme and the Beginnings of Cubism," p. 194.

harbor. As Seurat did in his Norman seascapes, van Rysselberghe surrounds the image with a narrow frame painted in the same technique, with Neo-Impressionist dots.

COLLIOURE

In the summer of 1905, the fishing village of Collioure made its own great impression on modern art. Collioure lies in the far southwest of France, where the Pyrenees come down to the Mediterranean. Not far from the Spanish border, it is different in spirit from the other seaside villages to the east along the French coast, for it stands at the crossroads of two cultures, French and Catalan. (At different times over the centuries, in fact, the region has changed hands between France and Spain.)

Matisse came to Collioure in mid-May of 1905, for a stay of nearly four months. Derain came to join him in July. Having successfully exhibited the Neo-Impressionist work *Luxe, calme et volupté* that March at the Salon des Indépendants in Paris, Matisse was now considered a leader of the avant-garde. *Luxe, calme et volupté*, of course, itself owed a debt to the South, for it was inspired by Matisse's stay in Saint-Tropez in the summer of the previous year.

In October of 1905, at the Salon d'automne, Matisse and Derain exhibited the works they had painted that summer in Collioure. This was the show that would lead to the coining of the label "Fauves" ("Wild beasts"), a response to the boldly unnatural color used by Matisse, Derain, and the artists around them. It was the light of Collioure, which Derain described as "a blond, golden light that eliminates shadows,"[31] that had led him and Matisse to handle color in the way they did. Derain's correspondence with Maurice de Vlaminck suggests that it was he who first became dissatisfied with the Neo-Impressionist technique that both artists were then exploring (the technique of *Luxe, calme et volupté*),[32] but it was Matisse who actually arrived at the new pictorial language. As in Neo-Impressionism, the Fauvist picture would be constructed primarily of color notations without dependence on drawn line. But where a Neo-Impressionist like Seurat or Signac would build the picture with methodical rigor as an even field of carefully calibrated colored dots, Matisse's Fauvist *Landscape at Collioure* (plate 68) appears more intuitive, the dots becoming marks that vary in size, shape, and orientation, and that cover the canvas irregularly, leaving patches of it bare.

Matisse painted few pictures that summer, and most of those he did paint were small sketches (plate 66) that he developed further after his return to Paris. *Landscape at Collioure* is one of these works. Here Matisse draws not with line but with a multitude of variegated color notations that record his response to the motif. In fact the motif itself is somewhat lost in the storm of bright-colored marks, unconstrained by linear design; there is little sense of a specific location. Unpainted areas of the canvas bring out the luminosity of the color, suggesting a dazzling light, pulsating with energy. This intense color, liberated from purely descriptive or imitative purpose, lies in an almost abstract pattern of irregular patches and strokes. Fauvism was a moment of liberation from earlier approaches to color and composition, yet works like *Landscape at Collioure* also contain an element of the classical tradition: this is a timeless arcadian landscape, a kind of visual paradise.

Derain may have stimulated Matisse's reaction against Neo-Impressionism, but in making the same kind of departure he himself moved in a different direction; his own Fauve works are entirely different in style from those of Matisse. The colors of *Fishing Boats, Collioure* (plate 67) are dazzlingly bright, but they are applied in more uniform strokes than Matisse uses in *Landscape at Collioure*, and in larger flat planes. In this respect the work recalls Gauguin, whose late paintings of Oceania Matisse and Derain probably saw that summer during a visit to Gauguin's friend Daniel de Monfreid. Derain's works are also keyed more closely to specific scenes and views, and are more traditional in composition. At the high horizon line of *Fishing Boats, Collioure*, signs of the port are clearly visible. This strong horizontal line reechoes in the horizontal marks stacked like bricks to suggest distant waves, and is countered by the near-verticals and diagonals in the masts of the boats. The result is a vibrant, light-suffused seascape, bold and intense. Shocking as they seemed when exhibited at the Salon d'automne, works like this one placed Derain among the major figures of the Paris avant-garde. Inspired by the landscape, color, and light of Collioure, he and Matisse had arrived at a new confidence in the power of contrasting colors, and in color as the agent of pictorial composition.

31. Derain, letter to Vlaminck, summer 1905, in *Lettres à Vlaminck*, p. 148.

32. Derain, letter to Vlaminck, summer 1905, in ibid., pp. 146–47.

PLATE 42. Paul Cézanne. ***Reeds at Jas de Bouffan.*** 1880–82. Watercolor and pencil on paper, 18 ⅝ x 12 ⅛" (47.2 x 30.8 cm). The Museum of Modern Art, New York. The William S. Paley Collection

FIGURE 44. Allée of chestnut trees at Jas de Bouffan, Aix-en-Provence, c. 1935. John Rewald Library Collection, Archives of the National Gallery of Art, Washington, D.C.

FIGURE 45. Bridge at Gardanne, c. 1935. John Rewald Library Collection, Archives of the National Gallery of Art, Washington, D.C.

PLATE 43. Paul Cézanne. *The Bridge at Gardanne.* 1885–86. Watercolor and pencil on paper, 8 $^1/_8$ x 12 $^1/_4$" (20.6 x 31.1 cm). The Museum of Modern Art, New York. Lillie P. Bliss Collection

PLATE 44. Paul Cézanne. *Foliage.*
1895–1900. Watercolor and pencil on
paper, 17 5/8 x 22 3/8" (44.8 x 56.8 cm). The
Museum of Modern Art, New York. Lillie
P. Bliss Collection

FIGURE 46. Rocks near the cave above
Château Noir, Aix-en-Provence, c. 1935. John
Rewald Library Collection, Archives of the
National Gallery of Art, Washington, D.C.

PLATE 45. Paul Cézanne. ***Rocks near the
Caves above Le Château Noir (Rochers
près des grottes au-dessus du Château
Noir).*** 1895–1900. Watercolor and pencil
on paper, 12 1/8 x 18 3/4" (31.7 x 47.6 cm).
The Museum of Modern Art, New York.
Lillie P. Bliss Collection

FIGURE 47. Château Noir, Aix-en-Provence, c. 1935. John Rewald Library Collection, Archives of the National Gallery of Art, Washington, D.C.

PLATE 46. Paul Cézanne. *Le Château Noir.* 1904–06. Oil on canvas, 29 x 36 ³/₄" (73.6 x 93.2 cm). The Museum of Modern Art, New York. Gift of Mrs. David M. Levy

FIGURE 48. Mont Sainte-Victoire, Aix-en-Provence, c. 1935. John Rewald Library Collection, Archives of the National Gallery of Art, Washington, D.C.

PLATE 47. Paul Cézanne. *Mont Sainte-Victoire.* 1902–06. Watercolor and pencil on paper, 16 3/4 x 21 3/8" (42.5 x 54.2 cm). The Museum of Modern Art, New York. Fractional gift of Mr. and Mrs. David Rockefeller (the donors retaining a life interest in the remainder)

PLATE 48. Paul Gauguin. **Washerwomen.**
1888. Oil on canvas, 29 7/8 x 36 1/4" (75.9 x
92.1 cm). The Museum of Modern Art,
New York. The William S. Paley Collection

PLATE 49. Edouard-Denis Baldus. **Roman Cemetery, Arles.** 1853. Salt print from a paper negative, 13 1/4 x 17 1/2" (33.6 x 44.5 cm). The Museum of Modern Art, New York. Gift of Harriette and Noel Levine and Anonymous Purchase Fund

PLATE 50. Vincent van Gogh. *The Olive Trees.* 1889. Oil on canvas, 28 5/8 x 36" (72.6 x 91.4 cm). The Museum of Modern Art, New York. Mrs. John Hay Whitney Bequest

FIGURE 49. Mont Gaussier, 1986

PLATE 51. Vincent van Gogh. **The Starry Night.** 1889. Oil on canvas, 29 x 36 ¹/₄" (73.7 x 92.1 cm). The Museum of Modern Art, New York. Acquired through the Lillie P. Bliss Bequest

FIGURE 50. Saint-Rémy-de-Provence from the air, with the Saint-Paul-du-Mausole asylum in the foreground, c. 1940s. Postcard

FIGURE 51. Nice, n.d. Postcard

PLATE 52. Henri Matisse. **_Landscape._** 1918.
Oil on panel, 13 $\frac{1}{2}$ x 16 $\frac{1}{2}$" (34.2 x 41.9 cm).
The Museum of Modern Art, New York.
The William S. Paley Collection

PLATE 53. Louis Valtat. *Landscape.* 1904. Oil on canvas, 38 ¹/₂ x 51 ¹/₂" (97.7 x 130.8 cm). The Museum of Modern Art, New York. Gift of Mrs. Melville Wakeman Hall

FIGURE 52. Saint-Raphaël, view from the villa of Louis Valtat, 1999

PLATE 54 (ABOVE LEFT). Paul Signac. ***Port of Saint-Tropez (Port de Saint-Tropez)*** from the portfolio ***Album of Original Prints from the Vollard Gallery no. III (L'Album d'estampes originales de la Galerie Vollard no. III).*** 1898. Lithograph, comp: 17 1/4 x 13 1/8" (43.8 x 33.4 cm). The Museum of Modern Art, New York. Abby Aldrich Rockefeller Fund

PLATE 55 (ABOVE RIGHT). Paul Signac. ***The Buoy (Saint-Tropez Harbor) (La Bouée [Saint-Tropez: Le Port]).*** 1894. Lithograph, comp: 15 13/16 x 12 13/16" (40.2 x 32.5 cm). The Museum of Modern Art, New York. Abby Aldrich Rockefeller Fund

FIGURE 53. Port of Saint-Tropez, n.d. Postcard

PLATE 56. Henri Matisse. **Study for** ***Luxe,
calme et volupté.*** 1904. Oil on canvas,
12 7/8 x 16" (32.8 x 40.6 cm). The Museum
of Modern Art, New York. Mrs. John Hay
Whitney Bequest

PLATE 57. Eugène Atget. **Cannes. Umbrella Pines.** n.d. Albumen silver print, 8 ⁷/₁₆ x 6 ¹¹/₁₆" (21.5 x 17 cm). The Museum of Modern Art, New York. Abbott-Levy Collection. Partial gift of Shirley C. Burden

PLATE 58. Paul Cézanne. *L'Estaque.*
1882–83. Oil on canvas, 31 1/2 x 39" (80.3 x
99.4 cm). The Museum of Modern Art,
New York. The William S. Paley Collection

PLATE 59. André Derain. *L'Estaque.* 1906.
Oil on canvas, 13 7/8 x 17 3/4" (35.3 x 45.1 cm).
The Museum of Modern Art, New York.
Acquired through the Lillie P. Bliss Bequest

FIGURE 54. L'Estaque, n.d. Postcard

PLATE 60. André Derain. ***Bridge over the Riou.*** 1906. Oil on canvas, 32¹/₂ x 40" (82.5 x 101.6 cm). The Museum of Modern Art, New York. The William S. Paley Collection

FIGURE 55. L'Estaque, n.d. Postcard

PLATE 61. Georges Braque. ***The Great Trees, L'Estaque.*** 1906–07. Oil on canvas mounted on composition board, 31 ¹/₂ x 27 ³/₄" (80 x 70.5 cm). The Museum of Modern Art, New York. Fractional gift of Mr. and Mrs. David Rockefeller

Fig. 56. Bay of L'Estaque, 1984

PLATE 62. Georges Braque. **Road near**
L'Estaque. 1908. Oil on canvas, 23 $^3/_4$ x
19 $^3/_4$" (60.3 x 50.2 cm). The Museum of
Modern Art, New York. Given anonymously
(by exchange)

FIGURE 57. August Macke. **View of the Valley**
of the Riou. 1914. Photograph. Westfälisches
Landesmuseum für Kunst und
Kulturegeschichte, Münster

PLATE 63. Edouard-Denis Baldus. *La Ciotat.* Before 1859. Albumen silver print from a paper negative, 11 7/8 x 16 1/8" (30.2 x 41 cm). The Museum of Modern Art, New York. Gift of Paul F. Walter

PLATE 64. Georges Braque. ***Landscape at
La Ciotat.*** 1907. Oil on canvas, 28¹/₄ x 23³/₈"
(71.7 x 59.4 cm). The Museum of Modern Art,
New York. Acquired through the Katherine S.
Dreier and Adele R. Levy Bequests

FIGURE 58. Port of La Ciotat, n.d. Postcard

PLATE 65. Theo van Rysselberghe. **_The Port of Sète (Le Port de Cette)._** 1892. Oil on canvas, 21¹/₂ x 26" (54.5 x 66 cm). The Museum of Modern Art, New York. Estate of John Hay Whitney

FIGURE 59. Sète, n.d. Postcard

PLATE 66. Henri Matisse. ***Harbor at Collioure.*** 1907. Lithograph, comp: 4 5/16 x 7 5/8" (10.9 x 19.4 cm). The Museum of Modern Art, New York. Given in memory of Leo and Nina Stein

FIGURE 60. Port of Collioure, 1905. Archives Matisse

PLATE 67. André Derain. ***Fishing Boats, Collioure.*** 1905. Oil on canvas, 15 1/8 x 18 1/4" (38.2 x 46.3 cm). The Museum of Modern Art, New York. The Philip L. Goodwin Collection

FIGURE 61. Collioure, n.d. Postcard

PLATE 68. Henri Matisse. *Landscape at Collioure.* 1905. Oil on canvas, 15 1/4 x 18 3/8" (38.8 x 46.6 cm). The Museum of Modern Art, New York. Gift and Bequest of Mrs. Bertram Smith

LANDSCAPES ABROAD

HORTA DE EBRO, SPAIN

In the role of L'Estaque for Cézanne and Braque, or of Collioure for Matisse and Derain, stands the Catalan village of Horta de Ebro for Picasso. The works that the artist produced here in the summer of 1909 would play a crucial role in the evolution of Cubism.

Horta de Ebro (today known as Horta de San Juan) lies in the province of Tarragona, in Catalonia not far west of Barcelona. Its light is intense, its landscape rugged. Mountains rise above it; the earth and fields are pale silvery ocher and light green, the colors of Picasso's early Cubist pictures. Horta was the home village of Manuel Pallarés, a close friend of Picasso's from his youth in Spain, and he had visited it first in 1898, when he was sixteen years old. His return to Horta in 1909 turned out to be a productive and indeed crucial period in his work.[1]

In Paris that spring, Picasso had begun to depict the human figure in terms of large, faceted forms, as if it were a sculptural assemblage of geometric solids. At Horta over the summer, he applied the same principles to landscape, painting works such as *The Mill at Horta* (for which the Museum owns a study; plate 69), *Houses on the Hill, Horta de Ebro* (plate 70), and *The Reservoir, Horta de Ebro* (plate 71)—fully developed examples of Analytic Cubism.[2] Like Braque's paintings at L'Estaque in 1908, these works show Picasso's renewed interest in the methods of Cézanne, notably in their use of a high viewpoint and in the device of *passage*, whereby forms in different visual planes have open contours and bleed into each other. The visual structures of the paintings depend on angled, straight-edged forms, and suggest not so much pictorial depth as low relief; in fact Picasso reverses the principles of traditional one-point perspective, so that shapes seem to spill out toward the viewer rather than to recede into the distance as they get farther away. Evident in *Houses on the Hill*, this effect is still clearer in *The Reservoir*, where forms mass into a pyramidal structure that seems to move downward and outward toward the viewer, pushed forward by the back plane of the composition, which effectively blocks off the space.

Photographs Picasso took that summer (figs. 62 and 63) reveal that in some ways he depicted the architecture he saw in Horta quite closely (he may in fact have used the photographs as guides), but he altered the perspectives and the spatial relationships among the buildings. In *Houses on the Hill*, for example, he essentially combined separate points of view into a

1. On Picasso's visit to Horta see John Richardson, with the collaboration of Marilyn McCully, *The Painter of Modern Life*, vol. 2 of *A Life of Picasso* (New York: Random House, 1996), pp. 123–32.

2. For an extensive discussion of these works see William Rubin et al., *Picasso in the Collection of The Museum of Modern Art* (New York: The Museum of Modern Art, 1972), p. 56, and Maria Teresa Ocaña, *Picasso: Landscapes 1890-1912*, exh. cat. (Barcelona: Museu Picasso, 1994), pp. 283–85.

single image: the village is seen both from above and from below. Picasso's depictions of Horta are conceptual, ruled by an internal logic. This is true of paintings in general, of course, but Cubism brought a new rigor to a tendency we have observed throughout the art reproduced in this book, to abandon the illusion of mimetic depiction, the sense that the painting is a window on the world. *The Mill at Horta* and *The Reservoir* ask us to think not so much of an actual place as of a composition of regular forms modeled in low relief, with ochers defining light and grays defining shadow. The clean planar geometry seen in these works would be a defining characteristic of Analytic Cubism, even as it grew more abstract in the years to come.

TANGIER, MOROCCO

In the decades around 1900, we have seen, the South of France exerted a magnetic pull on the modernist painters of the north. In January of 1912, Matisse went farther south still, following in the footsteps of Delacroix eighty years earlier and making the first of two trips to Morocco.[3] His visit—he stayed until mid-April—coincided with the signing of the Treaty of Fez, on March 30, 1912, which made Morocco officially a French protectorate. Elements of life in Tangier during this period must have been heavily influenced by French culture, and familiar to Matisse; but there was also the visual heritage of the Arab or Moorish history, not to mention the light and heat of North Africa.

Matisse's visit to Morocco was clearly very rich, and left a deep impression on his work. Many years later, in a letter to his publisher Tériade of July 1951, he claimed that travel had essentially given him nothing except a new perception of light, but added, "The voyages to Morocco helped me...make contact with nature again better than did the application of a lively but somewhat limiting theory, Fauvism. I found the landscapes of Morocco just as they had been described in the paintings of Delacroix and in Pierre Loti's novels. One morning in Tangiers I was riding in a meadow; the flowers came up to the horse's muzzle. I wondered where I had already had a similar experience—it was in reading one of Loti's descriptions in his book *Au Maroc*."[4]

Matisse had visited Algeria in 1906, and had subsequently begun looking carefully at African art and had seen exhibitions of Islamic art (at the Musée des Arts Decoratifs, Paris, in 1907, and then in Munich in 1910). He had become increasingly interested in the traditions of the decorative arts, and after 1908 he had begun painting large compositions in which he tried to unite the harmonious well-being of the decorative with the philosophically ambitious traditions of painting. His stay in Morocco catalyzed this interest, and in the group of Moroccan landscapes that includes *Periwinkles/Moroccan Garden (Les Pervenches/Jardin marocain*; plate 72), he tried to combine elements of the nature he saw in North Africa with the use of a decorative, arabesque line to organize the pictorial surface.[5] In an interview of 1925, Matisse remarked, "Slowly, I discovered the secret of my art. It consists of a meditation on nature, on the expression of a dream, which is always inspired by reality."[6] As in earlier works such as the Neo-Impressionist canvas *Luxe, calme et volupté* (1904–05; fig. 8) and the Fauvist *Bonheur de vivre* (1905–06; fig. 9), Matisse tried in his Moroccan paintings to convey both the dream and the real.

When Matisse arrived in Morocco, he intended to work on two landscapes commissioned by a patron, the Moscow merchant Ivan Morozov. He may for a while have intended *Periwinkles/Moroccan Garden* to be one of these works. The picture was painted sometime between late February and April 1, 1912, in the garden of a villa belonging to a Scottish expatriate, Jock Brooks. The Villa Brooks lay in a part of Tangier inhabited by wealthy Europeans, and the garden was very striking: "It was immense," Matisse would remember, "with meadows as far as the eye can see. I worked in a part which was planted with very large trees, whose foliage spread very high. The ground was covered with acanthus."[7] In fact Matisse painted a canvas titled *Acanthus* (*Les Acanthes*; Moderna Museet, Stockholm) during his stay in Tangier, and *Periwinkles/Moroccan Garden*, *Acanthus*, and a third work, *La Palme* (National Gallery, Washington, D.C.), together seem to make up a stylistic trio.

All of these works combine observation and decorativeness in compositions of sumptuous color. *Periwinkles* was methodically planned; an under-drawing in pencil, which remains quite visible, was then followed in paint. Matisse uses large areas of unmodulated color, devoid of incidental detail, and unifies them with swirling arabesque lines. These arabesques link the work to the Orientalist tradition, as does the sense of lush, tropical vegetation, and the color scheme—the thin layers of salmon pinks, the light and dark greens, the ochers, and the touches of periwinkle blue, all suffused with light and mellowness. The composition is almost abstract in its interplay of hard-to-identify colored shapes. As landscape it is non-specific, another of Matisse's personal visions of a timeless Arcadia, yet it is at the same time based on a real place that must actually have seemed to the artist an exotic paradise. Once again, a new locale had produced a new modern vision of landscape.

3. On Henri Matisse's visits to Morocco see Jack Cowart et al., *Matisse in Morocco: The Paintings and Drawings, 1912–1913*, exh. cat. (Washington, D.C.: National Gallery of Art, 1990).

4. Matisse, in "Matisse Speaks," *Matisse on Art*, ed. Jack D. Flam (London: Phaidon, 1973), p. 132.

5. *Periwinkles/Moroccan Garden* is discussed in depth in *Matisse in Morocco*, cat. 6, p. 70.

6. Matisse, in *Matisse on Art*, p. 55.

7. Matisse, quoted in *Matisse in Morocco*, p. 68.

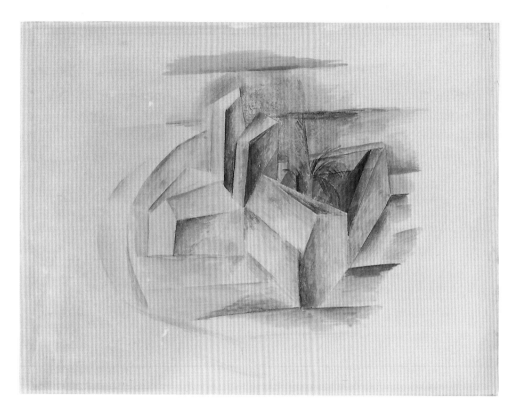

PLATE 69. Pablo Picasso. **Study for *The Mill at Horta.*** 1909. Watercolor on paper, 9 ³/₄ x 15" (24.8 x 38.2 cm). The Museum of Modern Art, New York. The Joan and Lester Avnet Collection

FIGURE 62. Pablo Picasso. ***View of Horta de Ebro.*** 1909. Photograph. Archives Picasso, Paris

PLATE 70. Pablo Picasso. **Houses on the Hill, Horta de Ebro.** 1909. Oil on canvas, 25 $^5/_8$ x 31 $^7/_8$" (65 x 81 cm). The Museum of Modern Art, New York. Nelson A. Rockefeller Bequest

PLATE 71. Pablo Picasso. ***The Reservoir, Horta de Ebro.*** 1909. Oil on canvas, 24¹/₈ x 20¹/₈" (61.5 x 51.1 cm). The Museum of Modern Art, New York. Fractional gift of Mr. and Mrs. David Rockefeller

FIGURE 63. Pablo Picasso. ***Roofs at Horta de Ebro.*** 1909. Photograph. Archives Picasso, Paris

PLATE 72 (OPPOSITE). Henri Matisse. ***Periwinkles/Moroccan Garden (Les Pervenches/Jardin Morocain).*** 1912. Oil, pencil, and charcoal on canvas, 48 x 32¹/₄" (116.8 x 82.5 cm). The Museum of Modern Art, New York. Gift of Florene M. Schoenborn

SELECTED BIBLIOGRAPHY

Benjamin, Roger. "The Decorative Landscape: Fauvism and the Arabesque of Observation." *Art Bulletin* 75 (June 1993): 295–316.

Bezucha, R. "Being Realistic about Realism." In G. P. Weisberg, ed. *The European Realist Tradition.* Bloomington: Indiana University Press, 1982.

Bomford, David, et al. *Impressionism: Art in the Making.* New Haven and London: Yale University Press, 1990.

Bouret, Jean. *The Barbizon School and 19th Century French Landscape Painting.* Greenwich, Conn.: New York Graphic Society, 1973.

Boyle-Turner, Caroline. *The Prints of the Pont-Aven School: Gauguin and His Circle in Brittany.* Washington, D.C.: Smithsonian Institution Press, 1986.

———. *Gauguin et l'école de Pont-Aven.* Exh. cat. Paris: Bibliothèque Nationale, 1989.

Braudel, Fernand. *History and Environment.* Vol. 1 of *The Identity of France.* Trans. Siân Reynolds. New York: Harper and Row, 1988.

Brettell, R. R. *A Day in the Country: Impressionism and the French Landscape.* Exh. cat. Los Angeles: Los Angeles County Museum of Art, 1984.

———. *Pissarro and Pontoise: The Painter in a Landscape.* New Haven and London: Yale University Press, 1990.

Buzard, James. *The Beaten Track: European Tourism, Literature, and Ways to Culture, 1800–1918.* Oxford: at the University Press, 1994.

Camp, Maxime du. *Le Salon de 1861.* Paris, 1861.

Castagnary, Jules-Antoine. *Salons (1857–1870).* With a preface by Eugène Spuller. Paris: Bibliothèque-Charpentier, 1892.

Champa, K. S., et al. *The Rise of Landscape Painting in France: Corot to Monet.* Exh. cat. Manchester, N.H.: Currier Gallery of Art, 1991.

Chassey, Eric de. "Braque et la leçon de l'Estaque." *Beaux Arts* no. 125 (July/August 1994): 56–68.

Clark, M. *Lighting Up the Landscape: French Impressionism and Its Origins.* Exh. cat. Edinburgh: National Gallery of Scotland, 1986.

Clark, T. J. *The Painting of Modern Life: Paris in the Art of Manet and His Followers.* New York: Alfred A. Knopf, 1985.

Coke, Van Deren. *The Painter and the Photograph.* Exh. cat. Albuquerque: University of New Mexico Press, 1964.

Cole, Henri. "Point of Views." *Art and Antiques* 8 (Summer 1991): 70–73.

Cosgrove, D., and S. Daniels, eds. *The Iconography of Landscape.* Cambridge: at the University Press, 1988.

Cowart, Jack, and Dominique Fourcade. *Henri Matisse: The Early Years in Nice, 1916–1930.* Exh. cat. Washington, D.C.: National Gallery of Art, and New York: Harry N. Abrams, 1986.

Cowart, Jack, et al. *Matisse in Morocco: The Paintings and Drawings, 1912–1913.* Exh. cat. Washington, D.C.: National Gallery of Art, 1990.

Culler, Jonathan. "The Semiotics of Tourism." In *Framing the Sign: Criticism and Its Institutions.* Oxford: at the University Press, 1988.

Derain, André. *Lettres à Vlaminck.* Ed. Maurice de Vlaminck. Paris: Flammarion, 1955.

Dornic, Alain. *Des Baous à la Méditerranée.* Cagnes-sur-Mer: Edica, 1983.

Elderfield, John. *Matisse in the Collection of The Museum of Modern Art.* Exh. cat. Nyew York: The Museum of Modern Art, 1978.

———. *Henri Matisse: A Retrospective.* Exh. cat. New York: The Museum of Modern Art, 1992.

Flam, Jack. *Matisse: The Man and His Art, 1869–1918.* Ithaca: Cornell University Press, 1986.

Freeman, Judi. *The Fauve Landscape.* Exh. cat. New York: Abbeville Press, and Los Angeles: Los Angeles County Museum of Art, 1990.

Georgel, Pierre. *Monet: Le Cycle des "Nymphéas".* Exh. cat. Paris: Musée national de l'Orangerie, 1999.

Gombrich, E. H. *Studies in the Art of the Renaissance.* London: Phaidon, 1966.

Grad, B. L., and T. A. Riggs. *Visions of City and Country: Prints and Photographs of Nineteenth-Century France.* Worcester, Mass.: Worcester Art Museum, 1980.

Green, Nicholas. *The Spectacle of Nature: Landscape and Bourgeois Culture in 19th Century France.* Manchester: at the University Press, 1990.

Hamilton, V. *Boudin at Trouville.* Glasgow: Glasgow Museums, 1992.

Henri Matisse, 1904–1917. Exh. cat. Paris: Centre Georges Pompidou/Musée d'art moderne, 1993.

Herbert, James D. *Fauve Painting: The Making of Cultural Politics.* New Haven: Yale University Press, 1992.

Herbert, Robert L. *Barbizon Revisited.* Exh. cat. New York: Clarke & Way, 1962.

——. "City vs. Country: The Rural Image in French Painting from Millet to Gauguin." *Artforum* 8 no. 6 (February 1970): 44–55.

——. "Method and Meaning in Monet." *Art in America* 67 no. 5 (September 1979): 90–108.

——. *Impressionism: Art, Leisure and Parisian Society.* New Haven and London: Yale University Press, 1988.

——. *Monet on the Normandy Coast: Tourism and Painting, 1867–1886.* New Haven and London: Yale University Press, 1994.

Herbert, Robert L., with Françoise Cachin et al. *Georges Seurat, 1859–1891.* Exh. cat. New York: The Metropolitan Museum of Art, 1991.

House, John. *Monet: Nature into Art.* New Haven and London: Yale University Press, 1986.

House, John, with contributions by Anne Dumas, Jane Mayo Roos, and James F. McMillan. *Landscapes of France: Impressionism and Its Rivals.* Exh. cat. London: Hayward Gallery, 1995.

Ives, Colta Feller. *The Great Wave: The Influence of Japanese Woodcuts on French Prints.* New York: The Metropolitan Museum of Art, 1974.

Jeanniot, Georges. "Souvenirs sur Degas." *Revue Universelle* LV nos. 14 (October 15, 1933) and 15 (November 1, 1933).

Kendall, Richard. *Degas Landscapes.* New Haven and London: Yale University Press, 1993.

Kendall, Richard, ed. *Cézanne and Poussin: A Symposium.* Sheffield: Academic Press, 1993.

Ladurie, Emmanuel Le Roy. *Paysages: L'Art et la terre en Europe du moyen age au xxe siècle.* Exh. cat. Paris: Bibliothèque nationale de France, 1994.

Lanquar, Robert. *Sociologie du tourisme et des voyages.* Paris: Presses Universitaires de France, 1985.

Lassaigne, Jacques. "Entretiens avec Braque." In *Les Cubistes.* Exh. cat. Bordeaux: Musée des Beaux-Arts, 1973.

L'Estaque: Naissance du paysage moderne 1870–1910. Exh. cat. Marseilles: Musées de Marseille, Réunions des Musées Nationaux, 1994.

Le Paysage provençal avant l'impressionisme (1845–1874). Exh. cat. Toulon: Musée de Toulon, 1992.

Les Sites Cézanniens du pas d'Aix: Hommage à John Rewald. Paris: Réunion des Musées Nationaux, 1996.

Leymarie, Jean. *Mediterranée: Sources et formes du xxe siècle.* Paris: Artcurial, 1988.

Loyrette, Henri, and Gary Tinterow. *Origins of Impressionism.* New York: The Metropolitan Museum of Art, 1994.

Machotka, Paul. *Cézanne: Landscape into Art.* New Haven: Yale University Press, 1996.

Matisse, Henri. *Matisse on Art.* Ed. Jack D. Flam. London: Phaidon, 1973.

Merriman, J. M., ed. *French Cities in the Nineteenth Century.* London: Hutchinson, 1982.

Mitchell, Claudine. "Time and the Idea of Patriarchy in the Pastorals of Puvis de Chavannes." *Art History* 10 (June 1987): 187–202.

Mitchell, W. J. T., ed. *Landscape and Power.* Chicago: at the University Press, 1994.

Moffett, Charles S., et al. *The New Painting: Impressionism, 1874–1886.* San Francisco: The Museums, 1986.

Monet's Years at Giverny: Beyond Impressionism. Exh. cat. New York: The Metropolitan Museum of Art, 1978.

Moureau, François. *L'Oeil aux aguets, ou, L'Artiste en voyage: Etudes réunis.* Paris: Klincksieck, 1995.

Nochlin, Linda, ed. *Impressionism and Post-Impressionism, 1874–1904: Sources and Documents.* Englewood Cliffs, N.J.: Prentice Hall, 1966.

Nora, Pierre. *Realms of Memory: Rethinking the French Past.* Ed. Lawrence D. Kritzman. Trans. Arthur Goldhammer. New York: Columbia University Press, 1996.

Ocaña, Maria Teresa, et. al. *Picasso: Landscapes 1890–1912.* Barcelona: Museu Picasso, 1994.

Orr, Lynn Federle. *Monet: Late Painting of Giverny from the Musée Marmotton.* New York: Harry N. Abrams, 1994.

Orwicz, M. "Criticism and Representations of Brittany in the Early Third Republic." *Art Journal* 46 (Winter 1987).

Pearce, Douglas G., and Richard W. Butler, ed. *Tourism Research: Critiques and Challenges.* London: Routledge, in association with the International Academy for the Study of Tourism, 1993.

Peintres de la couleur en Provence 1875–1920. Exh. cat. Paris: Réunion des Musées Nationaux, 1995.

Picard, Denis. "Une Région pour la peinture." *Connaissance-des-Arts* no. 515 (March 1995): 124–29.

Pickvance, Ronald. *Van Gogh in Saint Rémy and Anvers.* Exh. cat. New York: The Metropolitan Museum of Art, 1986.

Pinkney, David H. *Napoleon III and the Rebuilding of Paris.* Princeton: at the University Press, 1958.

Pollock, Griselda. "Van Gogh and the Poor Slaves: Images of Rural Labour as Modern Art." *Art History* 11 (September 1988): 407–32.

Prendergast, C. *Paris and the Nineteenth Century.* Oxford: at the University Press, 1992.

Pugh, S., ed. *Reading Landscape: Country-City-Capital.* Manchester: at the University Press, 1990.

Quigley, T. R. "Shooting at the Father's Corpse: The Feminist Art Historian as Producer." *The Journal of Aesthetics and Art Criticism* 52 (Fall 1994): 407–13.

Reff, Theodore. "Cézanne and Poussin." *Journal of the Warburg and Courtauld Institutes* 23 (1960): 150–74.

Rewald, John. *The History of Impressionism.* 1946. Fourth ed. New York: The Museum of Modern Art, 1973.

———. "The Last Motifs at Aix." In William Rubin, ed. *Cézanne: The Late Work.* Exh. cat. New York: The Museum of Modern Art, 1977.

———. *Post-Impressionism: From van Gogh to Gauguin.* 1956. Third ed. New York: The Museum of Modern Art, 1978.

Rewald, John, ed. *Paul Cézanne: Letters.* London: Bruno Cassirer, 1941.

Rewald, John, in collaboration with Walter Feilchenfeldt and Jayne Warman. *The Paintings of Paul Cézanne: A Catalogue Raisonné.* New York: Harry N. Abrams, 1996.

Richardson, John, with the collaboration of Marilyn McCully. *The Painter of Modern Life.* Vol. 2 of *A Life of Picasso.* New York: Random House, 1996.

Ringer, Greg, ed. *Destinations: Cultural Landscapes of Tourism.* London: Routledge, 1998.

Robinson, William H. "Puvis de Chavannes's Summer and the Symbolist Avant-Garde." *The Bulletin of the Cleveland Museum of Art* 78 (January 1991): 2–27.

Rosenblum, Naomi. *A World History of Photography.* New York, London, and Paris: Abbeville Press, 1997.

Rubin, William, ed. *Cézanne: The Late Work.* Exh. cat. New York: The Museum of Modern Art, 1977.

Rubin, William S., and Matthew Armstrong. *The William S. Paley Collection.* Exh. cat. New York: The Museum of Modern Art, 1996.

Rubin, William, et al. *Picasso in the Collection of The Museum of Modern Art.* New York: The Museum of Modern Art, 1972.

Shaw, Jennifer. "Imagining the Motherland: Puvis de Chavannes, Modernism, and the Fantasy of France." *Art History* 79 (December 1987): 586–610.

Shiff, Richard. *Cézanne and the End of Impressionism: A Study of the Theory, Technique and Critical Evaluation of Modern Art.* Chicago: at the University Press, 1984.

Signac et la libération de la couleur: de Matisse à Mondrian. Exh. cat. Paris: Réunion des Musées Nationaux, 1997.

Soubiran, Jean-Roger. "Le Paysage provençal et l'école de Marseille avant l'impressionisme (1845–1874)." *Le Revue du Louvre et des Musées de France* 42 (December 1992): 143–44.

Szarkowski, John, and Maria Morris Hambourg. *The Art of Old Paris.* Vol. 2 of *The Work of Atget.* New York: The Museum of Modern Art, 1982.

Thomson, R. *Camille Pissarro: Impressionism, Landscape and Rural Labour.* London: South Bank Centre, 1990.

———. *Monet to Matisse: Landscape Painting in France 1874–1914.* Edinburgh: National Gallery of Scotland, 1994.

Tucker, P. H. *Monet at Argenteuil.* New Haven and London: Yale University Press, 1982.

Urry, John. *The Tourist Gaze: Leisure and Travel in Contemporary Societies.* London: Sage Publications, 1990.

Valenciennes, Pierre-Henri de. *Eléments de perspective practique à l'usage des artistes.* Paris, 1800. Reprint ed. Geneva: Minkoff, 1973.

Varnedoe, Kirk. *Masterpieces from the David and Peggy Rockefeller Collection: Manet to Picasso.* Exh. cat. New York: The Museum of Modern Art, 1994.

Varnedoe, Kirk, et al. *Masterworks from the Louise Reinhardt Smith Collection.* Exh. cat. New York: Museum of Modern Art, 1995.

Verdi, Richard. *Cézanne and Poussin: The Classical Vision of Landscape.* Exh. cat. Edinburgh: National Gallery of Scotland, 1990.

Volkmar, Karl F. "A Natural Order: Observation and the Four Seasons." *Art Criticism* 13 no. 1 (1998): 22–40.

Wayne, Kenneth. *Impressions of the Riviera: Monet, Renoir, Matisse, and Their Contemporaries.* Exh. cat. Portland, Me.: Portland Museum of Art, 1998.

Weber, E. *Peasants into Frenchmen: The Modernization of Rural France, 1870–1914.* London: Chatto and Windus, 1977.

Wintermute, A., ed. *Claude to Corot: The Development of Landscape Painting in France.* New York: Colnaghi, 1990.

Yiorgos Apostolopoulos, Stella. *The Sociology of Tourism: Theoretical and Empirical Investigations.* London and New York: Routledge, 1996.

INDEX OF PLATES

PHOTOGRAPH CREDITS